T0319011

Cambridge Elements ≣

Elements in the Global Middle Ages
edited by
Geraldine Heng
University of Texas at Austin
Susan Noakes
University of Minnesota, Twin Cities

SOUTHEAST ASIAN INTERCONNECTIONS

Geography, Networks and Trade

Derek Heng
Northern Arizona University

CAMBRIDGE
UNIVERSITY PRESS

Shaftesbury Road, Cambridge CB2 8EA, United Kingdom

One Liberty Plaza, 20th Floor, New York, NY 10006, USA

477 Williamstown Road, Port Melbourne, VIC 3207, Australia

314–321, 3rd Floor, Plot 3, Splendor Forum, Jasola District Centre,
New Delhi – 110025, India

103 Penang Road, #05–06/07, Visioncrest Commercial, Singapore 238467

Cambridge University Press is part of Cambridge University Press & Assessment,
a department of the University of Cambridge.

We share the University's mission to contribute to society through the pursuit of
education, learning and research at the highest international levels of excellence.

www.cambridge.org
Information on this title: www.cambridge.org/9781108827423

DOI: 10.1017/9781108907095

First published 2022

A catalogue record for this publication is available from the British Library.

ISBN 978-1-108-82742-3 Paperback
ISSN 2632-3427 (online)
ISSN 2632-3419 (print)

Southeast Asian Interconnections

Geography, Networks and Trade

Elements in the Global Middle Ages

DOI: 10.1017/9781108907095
First published online: December 2022

Derek Heng
Northern Arizona University

Author for correspondence: Derek Heng, derek.heng@nau.edu

Abstract: Since the late first millennium CE, Maritime Southeast Asia has been an interconnected zone, with its societies and states maintaining economic and diplomatic relations with both China and Japan to the east and the Indian subcontinent and Middle East to the west. This global connectedness was facilitated by merchant and shipping networks that originated from within and outside Southeast Asia, resulting in a transregional economy developing by the early second millennium CE. Sojourning populations began to appear in Maritime Southeast Asia, culminating in records of Chinese and Indian settlers in such places as Sumatra, the Malay Peninsula and the Gulf of Siam by the mid-first millennium CE. At the same time, information about products that were harvested in Southeast Asia began to be appropriated by pockets of society in China, India and the Middle East, resulting in the production of new knowledge of and uses for these products in these markets.

Keywords: Southeast Asia, commercial networks, shipping and trade, economic integration, trade products

ISBNs: 9781108827423 (PB), 9781108907095 (OC)
ISSNs: 2632-3427 (online), 2632-3419 (print)

Contents

1 Introduction: Southeast Asia in the Global Middle Ages

Throughout history, Southeast Asia has been an important region in Maritime Asia. Located between the Indian Ocean and the Pacific Ocean, the region served as the maritime connection between the littoral regions of the east Pacific Rim, as well as between continental Asia and Australasia. These maritime connections were supplemented on land via connections between the northeast Indian subcontinent and south China. Land routes connected northeastern India and Bangladesh with Myanmar and thence to Yunnan and Sichuan Provinces in China. Overland routes also connected the hills of north Mainland Southeast Asia, including present-day Laos and north Vietnam, with southern China.

The result has been that, throughout history, Southeast Asia has played an integral role as the nexus of human interaction and exchange, initially across the Old World and by the sixteenth century across the globe as well. However, unlike other interstitial spaces known in world history, such as central Asia, whose urban centers served primarily as nodal points along the conduit of human movement between larger bastions of societies and economies, Southeast Asia has been an economic region in its own right. Its geographical location, and the resources that it possessed as a result of its diverse ecologies and geology, have meant that it has served as a source of diverse products that could be extracted from its natural environment.

This Element seeks to understand Southeast Asia's economic history within the broader context of a Global Middle Ages. The phrase "Global Middle Ages" may, at first glance, be regarded as somewhat anachronistic in the context of Southeast Asian historiography. The term's Eurocentric origins seem initially in complete contradiction to the trajectory of Southeast Asian scholarship, which has, since the 1960s, embodied a deep philosophical underpinning in autonomous histories as a means of repudiating centuries of colonialism and western-centrism that characterized studies of classical Southeast Asian societies and cultures (Smail, 1961). Nonetheless, the parameters of the "Middle Ages," as they have been understood and applied in European historiography, can be usefully applied to the periodization of Southeast Asian history, which has hitherto been recognized by historians as vital to our understanding of the region's societies in the early modern and modern eras, but is not yet fully elaborated for the eras before European incursion as a distinct period in its own right. For the purposes of this Element, I will refer to this precolonial period before the advent of modernity in terms of a Global Middle Ages as well as premodern time and premodernity.

As a period characterized by the decline of large transregional empires of the axial age (Mullins et al., 2018), premodernity, for Southeast Asia, began with the demise of the Persian or Achaemenid Empire (550–330 BCE), Roman Empire (27 BCE–CE 476), the Han Dynasty in China (206 BCE–CE 220) and the Mauryan Empire of India (322–185 BCE). In place of these transregional empires were large political entities, or first-tier states, each substantial in their own right but not necessarily occupying geographical spaces that traversed a diversity of ecological zones that came with a diversity of locational latitude and climate and geological zones as the transregional empires did, and therefore not being able to be economically self-sufficient. The result was that these large states, while economically well-to-do, often had to reach beyond their respective borders to engage in trade in order to garner a similar richness of material culture as that witnessed in the axial age empires. The post-axial age was hence characterized by sizeable first-tier states that maintained vibrant transregional interactions with each other over both land and sea. Consequently, an increase in international commerce, material exchanges and cultural interactions occurred, as these societies and economies sought to increase their levels of affluence. This drive outward was supported by state-sponsored commercial institutions and networks, and the concomitant movement of people across regions led to cultural exchanges and transferences across spaces. First-tier states that flourished during this era included the Sassanid Dynasty and the Umayyad and Abbasid Caliphates in the Middle East, Levant and North Africa; the Tang (618–907 CE) and Song (960–1278 CE) Dynasties in China and east central Asia; and the Gupta (240–550 CE), Pandyan (third century BCE–fourteenth century CE) and Chola (848–1279 CE) Dynasties on the Indian subcontinent.

Additionally, an environmental consideration has to be made for this period as well. The Global Middle Ages corresponded to the Medieval Warm Period, when, between the ninth and thirteenth centuries, the Northern Hemisphere in particular experienced longer summers while, for certain regions of the world, more rainfall occurred. The result was that larger tracts of land, including areas that used to not be arable, such as the higher altitude areas of the Alps in Europe, became available for agricultural activities. Overall agricultural output by human societies throughout the Northern Hemisphere increased, leading to an expansion in the economy and the ability to sustain larger populations than before. This additional agrarian output contributed to an increase in overall disposable income, which in turn fueled international trade as the levels and degrees of sophistication of consumption by human societies across the world, and in Asia in particular, rose significantly.

During Southeast Asia's Middle Age, roughly corresponding to the mid-first to mid-second millennium CE (Figure 1), the region was marked by the rise of important regional powers that were engaged with the world. In Mainland Southeast Asia, the Khmer Empire rose in the ninth century to establish its hold over much of present-day Cambodia, south Vietnam and northeast Thailand for the next six centuries. In the Melaka Straits region, Srivijaya (650–1275), a thalassocracy centered at the city of Palembang (present-day southeast Sumatra), extended its influence over much of the coastal regions of Sumatra, the Malay Peninsula and Isthmus of Kra, and northeast Java from the seventh to the thirteenth century. In the Indonesian archipelago, various agrarian societies, including Mataram, Singhasari and Kediri, rose in central and eastern Java, resulting in the rise of large agrarian states that maintained an economic complement of international trade both with the islands of the east Indonesian archipelago and with the other regional entities of Southeast Asia and Maritime Asia. Finally, the Pagan Kingdom extended its political rule over much of present-day Myanmar between the ninth and thirteenth centuries.

Together, these states were important players in the global economy. The vibrant economic interactions and movement of people also resulted in the exchange of cultural ideas and languages. While foreign communities were able to take root and develop at the nodal points of Southeast Asia's trade networks, some of the exogenous cultural traits were adopted and adapted to the local context. While the period prior to Southeast Asia's Middle Age was characterized predominantly by the importation and intraregional dissemination of material culture, such as beads, earthenware ceramics and bronze items (Carter, 2015 & 2016; Francis, 1990 & 1991; Higham, 1996; Miksic, 2003), the Middle Age was characterized by adoption, assimilation and exportation of not just material culture and its attendant consumption practices but also other facets of society, including religion, statecraft, social organization, architecture and aesthetics.

The vibrant economic and social interactions that characterized this period of Southeast Asian history came to an end only with the introduction of European economic mercantilism in Maritime Asia from the sixteenth century onwards, first by the Spanish crown and Portuguese Estado da India in the Philippines and Melaka respectively, followed by the Dutch in the Indonesian archipelago in the seventeenth century and the British by the nineteenth century (Irwin, 1991; Borschberg, 2004; Chaudhuri, 2006).

Several questions concerning Southeast Asia's role in the premodern period need answering. Firstly, how did this period in world history impact Southeast Asia in terms of its trade, the commercial networks that traversed the region and the products that it exported into the international economy? What was Southeast Asia's role in the transregional and global interactions that took place over this one-thousand-year period? And how did these transregional economic interactions lead to the vestiges of economic integration between the different regions of Maritime Asia and the Old World, the way that Southeast

Figure 1 Map of Southeast Asia in the first millennium CE

Asia did later in the modern age of globalization in the nineteenth to early twenty-first century?

The purpose of this Element is to provide a précis of the role that Southeast Asia, located strategically between various civilizational cultures, played during this important period of world history. This role has not been incidental or passive but deliberate, and has capitalized on the natural environment and resources, coupled with the opportunities conferred by civilizational regions and first-tier states, to prosper economically and socially in a competitive international environment. The narrative will not only show that Southeast Asia's interactions were unique for the period in question but will also reflect recurring themes in the region's history through time.

This Element will comprise the following sections: (1) the geographical setting of Southeast Asia and its effects on international and regional interactions; (2) the shipping networks that operated across Southeast Asia; (3) the organized commercial networks that were active in the region; (4) the Southeast Asian products that were circulated in the global exchanges; and (5) the different facets of economic integration that developed as a result of Southeast Asia's role in the international commerce of this era.

2 Southeast Asia's Geography and Environment

Any study of Southeast Asia's economic history has to be firmly anchored in the importance of its geography and the role that this factor played in the development of trading networks, the products exchanged and the evolving nature of transregional economic integration in any period of history one would choose to examine.

Located at the nexus of the Bay of Bengal, Java Sea and South China Sea, Southeast Asia served, during the premodern and early modern eras, as the only maritime access for communications between the Indian Ocean littoral, Southeast Asia and East Asia. Through the Melaka Straits and Sunda Straits, the region has connected the societies and economies of East Africa, the Middle East, the Indian subcontinent, Southeast Asia, the Chinese landmass and the Japanese archipelago. A second maritime route from South Africa to Australia, located at forty degrees south of the equator and relying on the westerlies to make the crossing across the Indian Ocean from the Cape of Good Hope to western Australia, and thence from New Zealand across the Pacific Ocean to Cape Horn in South America, was discovered by European mariners only in the early seventeenth century. Even this route required the use of the Sunda Straits in order for ships to have access to Island Southeast Asia.

In the Age of Sail, transregional connections across Maritime Asia were made possible by two atmospheric phenomena. The first is the continental monsoon pattern (Figure 2). Generated by the heat over the continent of Asia during the summer months of the Northern Hemisphere and the relative warmth over the Indian Ocean during the summer months of the Southern Hemisphere, the seasonal warmth over the land and sea bodies leads to hot air rising, with cool air from the opposite hemisphere being drawn into the vacuum. This oscillating seasonal warmth creates monsoon winds blowing from the northeast (i.e. continental Asia) to the southwest (i.e. the Indian Ocean) between November and February. This is known as the northeast monsoon. Between April and September, the reverse phenomenon occurs, with the monsoon winds blowing from the southwest (i.e. the Indian Ocean) to the northeast (i.e. continental Asia). This is known as the southwest monsoon.

The annual oscillation of the monsoon winds has enabled mariners to sail back and forth across Maritime Asia throughout history. The northeast monsoon enabled vessels located in the northern areas of Maritime Asia to sail toward those located in the south, as well as laterally from east to west. As such, vessels located along the Chinese coast and Vietnamese coast of Mainland Southeast Asia, for example, would use the northeast monsoon to sail to Island Southeast Asia. Vessels located at the northern tip of Sumatra or the northwestern Malay Peninsula coastline would use the same monsoon to sail across the Bay of Bengal to the east coast of the Indian subcontinent, while those located along the west coast of India or the Arabian Sea would sail to the east coast of Africa. Vessels would sail in the opposite direction during the southwest monsoon season.

The second atmospheric phenomenon is the trade winds, or easterlies (Figure 3). These are the winds that blow year-round in a northeast to southwest direction north of the intertropical convergence zone (ITCZ), and southeast to northwest south of the ITCZ. The ITCZ, and therefore the easterlies, move north or south of the equator depending on the position of the sun vis-à-vis the equator. During the summer season of the Northern Hemisphere, the ITCZ moves north, as far as thirty degrees north in July. During the winter season of the Northern Hemisphere, the ITCZ moves south, as far as ten degrees south in January. The result is that, for Island Southeast Asia, the easterlies are an important factor for sail travel during the months of September to November. This is when the southwest trade winds, which blow in a clockwise circular pattern over this part of Southeast Asia, would enable vessels to sail in a circular direction across the region, from the eastern Indonesian archipelago to the west Java Sea, the southern end of the Melaka Straits and to North Borneo and the Sulu Archipelago.

The rhythm of the monsoons meant that passage between the west Indian Ocean and South China Sea littoral could occur predictably on an annual basis. The trade winds over Island Southeast Asia also enabled circulation within the maritime region of Southeast Asia. Consequently, Southeast Asia's location meant that, during the Age of Sail, the region was a natural convergence zone for ships utilizing the monsoons, resulting in the region's ports being the meeting places of vessels from East Asia through to the Middle East and East Africa. The trade winds in turn connected Island Southeast Asia to this

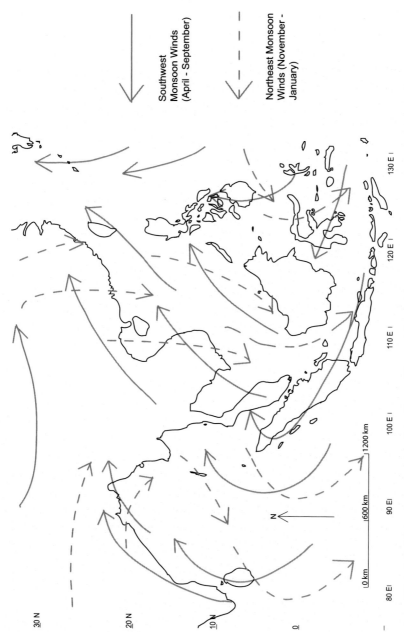

Southwest
Monsoon Winds
(April - September)

Northeast Monsoon
Winds (November -
January)

Figure 2 Monsoon patterns of the Bay of Bengal littoral, Maritime Southeast Asia and South China Sea

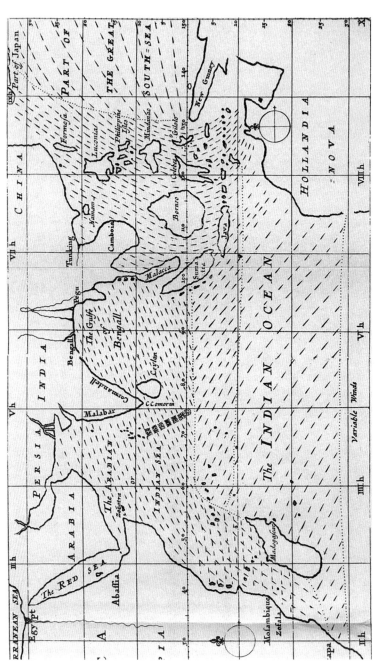

Figure 3 Section of *Map of the Trade Winds* (c.1686), by Edmond Halley, illustrating the trade winds over the Indian Ocean littoral and Maritime Southeast Asia between thirty degrees north and ten degrees south

(Source: Wikimedia Commons: https://commons.wikimedia.org/wiki/File:Edmond_Halley%27s_map_of_the_trade_winds,_1686.jpg)

international maritime system of sail during the months when the monsoon winds were not occurring. These factors have made Southeast Asia the heart of communications in Maritime Asia through time.

Southeast Asia's geography also had an impact on the products that it could offer to the international economy. Bounded by the Tropic of Cancer and the Tropic of Capricorn, Southeast Asia is a tropical zone. Coupled with its location in a maritime environment, this has resulted in the region being disposed to the rich flora and fauna resources that typically characterize tropical ecologies.

There are two main resource zones in Southeast Asia: (1) the maritime zone and (2) the land zone. Within the maritime zone, two areas may be noted. The first is the coastal areas along the seafront. Characterized by shores, mangroves and the numerous islets, shoals and outcrops that may be found in the seas of Southeast Asia (Figure 4), the coastal areas have been the source of marine resources for which the region has been known throughout history. These include such fauna and flora products as turtle carapaces, pearls, coral and cowrie shells, as well as seafood, such as seaweed and fish, to name a few. The seas have served as the conduits for communication and transport, both within Southeast Asia and to other parts of Maritime Asia. As such, the coastal areas have also served as launch points into this maritime communication space. The familiarity with the seas resulted, very early on, in the people who inhabited this area developing navigational expertise and shipbuilding techniques that have enabled them to travel and therefore connect Southeast Asia across large distances separated by seas. The habitation sites have also tended to be seasonal and mobile, with the inhabitants of these areas primarily living on watercraft and only sojourning on land occasionally when the need arises (Sopher, 1977; Chou, 2012).

The other area of the maritime zone is the riparian areas. Consisting of the banks along the lower reaches and river mouths of riverine systems and the coastal swales between the inland region and coastline, these areas have made available the natural resources that may be found within the catchment areas of the lower riverine systems, including such minerals as tin and gold, as well as the flora and fauna that thrive in this particular ecological zone, such as the sago palm, rattan and various hardwood timbers and aromatic woods. Additionally, the flooding of the coastal swales, resulting from the annual monsoon rains, has led to the development of seasonal coastal agriculture and the production of such cereals as rice as well as fruits, including coconuts. Finally, the proximity of the riparian areas to the coastline meant that the people of these areas were intimately connected to those inhabiting the coastal areas and were also able to communicate and interact with other riparian areas of Southeast Asia. The natural environment of these areas, coupled with the activities undertaken by the inhabitants, have resulted in more permanent habitation sites (Figure 5).

Figure 4 Photograph of mangrove along coastal Indonesia (c.1900), Leiden
University Library
(Source: Wikimedia Commons: https://commons.wikimedia.org/wiki/File:Mangroven_
aan_de_kust_in_Nederlands-Indi%C3%AB,_KITLV_95148.tiff)

The second zone in Southeast Asia – the land zone – is similarly distinguished by
two areas. The first is the floodplain areas. Located at a significant distance from the
sea, these areas include the floodplains of the major rivers of Southeast Asia, such
as the Brantas River delta in East Java, the plains of the Solo River in Central Java,
the plains of the Irrawaddy River in south and central Myanmar, the plains of the
Mekong River around the Tonle Sap at Angkor in central Cambodia (Figure 6) and
the Chao Praya River plains in south and central Thailand (Taylor, 1999; Mabbett
& Chandler, 1995; Stadtner & Freeman, 2013; Hudson & Lustig, 2008). The
floodplains have provided the basis for the development of agriculture and, early
on in history, the people inhabiting these inland areas developed agrarian societies
and their attendant social structures, including sophisticated state systems, and
urban settlement patterns and features, including fortified settlement sites, permanent urban features, such as walls, ramparts, roads and bridges, irrigation and
hydrological systems, as well as monumental architecture. The population bases
that these agrarian economies could sustain also resulted in their development of
manufactured products whose production required organized labor structures, such
as ceramics, textiles and metalwork (Hall, 2011a: 135–252).

The second area of the land zone is the inland and upland spaces. These consist
of inland areas that are at a higher elevation and therefore are not easily accessible

Figure 5 Photograph of a Malay settlement on the shore of Pulau Brani,
Singapore (c.1900)
(Source: Wikimedia Commons: https://commons.wikimedia.org/wiki/File:KITLV
_-_105809_-_Lambert_%26_Co.,_G.R._-_Singapore_-_Malay_village_on_the_island_
of_Pulau_Brani_near_Singapore_-_circa_1900.tif)

from the coast and riparian areas. They include the Barisan mountain range in
Sumatra (Figure 7), the hill regions of present-day Laos, northern Myanmar and
northern Vietnam, as well as the hill regions of Borneo Island and the Malay
Peninsula. These upland areas have been known as the sources of valuable
products unique to their natural environment, including such flora products as
camphor, wood-based aromatics and timbers, as well as minerals, such as gold
and tin, and semiprecious stones. The relative inaccessibility of these areas has
meant that, throughout history, the people inhabiting these areas have been
relatively isolated from the outside world, only periodically communicating
with the inhabitants of the plains and riparian areas that are connected to the
respective upland areas via a shared riverine system. External trade has also been
selective, being primarily centered on items that would have conferred prestige
on the leaders, as opposed to items of everyday use (Miksic, 2009; McKinnon,
2009; Hall, 2001; Salemink, 2008).

Taken together, Southeast Asia's resource zones have made available
a diverse range of products that could be introduced into the regional and global

Figure 6 Agricultural plains of Angkor, Siem Reap, Cambodia
(Source: Wikimedia Commons: https://commons.wikimedia.org/wiki/File:Angkor_
Area_(9731377014).jpg)

Figure 7 View of the forest of Bukit Barisan Mountain taken in Simalungun
Regency, north Sumatra, Indonesia
(Source: Wikimedia Commons: https://commons.wikimedia.org/wiki/File:
PEGUNUNGAN_BUKIT_BARISAN_DARI_SIPANGANBOLON
.jpg)

economies (Figure 8). These included flora products, such as spices, resins, aromatics woods and construction materials; agricultural products, such as rice, coconuts, sago and sugar; fauna products, such as rhinoceros horns, elephant tusks, hornbill casques, pelts, fish and sea cucumbers; minerals, such as tin, gold and arsenic; and manufactured items, such as textiles and ceramics (Wheatley, 1959). The respective availability of these products, and the extent of their demand, have been key determinants of their value and price in the regional and international trade systems.

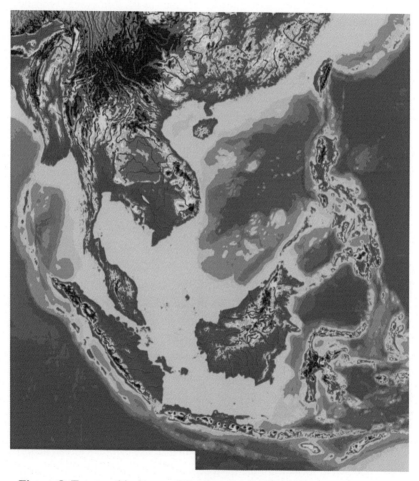

Figure 8 Topographical map of Southeast Asia, illustrating the upland areas
(yellow and red), plain areas (green) and riverine systems (blue)
(Source: Wikimedia Commons: https://commons.wikimedia.org/wiki/File:South_east_asia_
topographic_map.svg)

3 Southeast Asia's Shipping Networks during the Global Middle Ages

Prior to the Middle Ages in Maritime Asia, even though the abovementioned geographical factors were present, travel between the various littoral zones of Maritime Asia was still in its infancy. While there have been Indigenous wrecks dated to the first century CE excavated in Southeast Asia (Figure 9), exhibiting the possibility of open-sea voyaging both within and outside of the region, there has been little direct evidence of international shipping traversing Southeast Asia prior to the second half of the first millennium CE. Historical data has been confined to occasional mentions in Indic texts such as the Ramayana (Wheatley, 1961: 177–184; Devahuti, 1965: 11–13; Wheatley, 1964: 29–32) and in Ptolemy's *Geographia* (Wheatley, 1961, 123–176). In terms of archaeology, interactions between the Indian subcontinent and Southeast Asia have been confined to the presence of beads and south Indian ceramic ware in limited locations such as the east and west coasts of the Isthmus of Kra, and Funan, located at the Mekong River delta in present-day south Vietnam.

It is not until the third century CE that a more detailed record of the port city of Oc-Eo, in the kingdom of Funan, is available in the Chinese corpus. Concurrently, Indic inscriptions, as well as remains evidencing religious beliefs that originated outside of Southeast Asia and imported material culture, began to appear at Southeast Asian habitation sites of greater geographical distribution and at increasing frequency and intensity. Inscriptions in Pali and Sanskrit, for example, have been recovered at South Kedah (Malay Peninsula), Kutai (Borneo), Palembang (Sumatra) and Java, to name but a few (McKinnon, 2018; Bronkhorst, 2011; Daud, 2011). Indic-inspired religious architecture and art began to appear at such places as Champa (Lavy, 2003; Phuong, 2009), South Kedah (Jacq-Hergoualc'h, 2002: 472; Nik, 1994), Sri Kersetra (Myanmar) (Myo et al., 2017) and Prambanan (Java) (Ricklefs, 2010: 30–31). In the Chinese corpus, entries on several polities in Southeast Asia, including those located in Sumatra, Java, coastal Mainland Southeast Asia and Cambodia, begin to appear in the official histories of the southern Chinese kingdoms. Similarly, the Middle Eastern textual corpus also begins to contain information on several polities in the region.

This larger body of evidence of transregional interaction between Southeast Asia and the rest of Maritime Asia points to an increase in transregional flows of people, goods and ideas from the third century CE onward and coincides with the rise of the following states across Asia. In the Middle East, the Sassanid Dynasty (224–651) was in the ascendancy from the early third century, with the upward trajectory taken over initially by the Umayyad Caliphate (661–750) in the seventh century, followed by the Abbasid Caliphate (750–1258) from the eighth century onward. In the Indian subcontinent, the Gupta Dynasty (320–540) entered into its ascendancy in central and north India in the fourth century, while the Pallava Dynasty (275–897) was coming into its own in the south through the third century and the Chola Dynasty (848–1279) emerged as a significant state from the ninth century onward. Similarly, successive kingdoms in south China, centered at the administrative Yangzi delta city of Jiankang (modern-day Nanjing), lasted from the third to the sixth century. This was followed by the establishment of Sui (581–618) and Tang (618–907) rule over coastal south China from the late sixth through ninth centuries.

One of the characteristics important for Southeast Asia was that these states and societies had significant maritime cultures. South China, for example, had developed a number of riverine and coastal economies and societies by the mid-first millennium BCE, centered on the Yangzi River system and the rivers and delta areas along the South Chinese coastline. By the later Han period (21–220 CE), such port cities as Panyu (modern-day Guangzhou) had begun to engage in trade with Southeast Asia (Wang, 2003), while Jiankang, at the mouth of the Yangzi River delta, served as both the administrative and commercial center of successive south Chinese kingdoms during the Southern Dynasties period (220–589 CE) (Chittick, 2020). By the Tang period, south China had established a series of port cities along the south coast, including Yangzhou, Hangzhou, Mingzhou and Guangzhou. While, for much of the first millennium CE, China did not appear to have developed a large merchant marine that operated in Southeast Asia or the Indian Ocean, by the late eleventh century, changes instituted by the Song dynastic court to administrative policies governing international maritime trade resulted in the Chinese beginning to develop shipping networks into Southeast Asia and the Japanese archipelago (Heng, 2012: 48–51). Additional ports were also opened, including Quanzhou, which became the most important Chinese port city by the fourteenth century (So, 2000; Clark, 2002).

For the Middle East, maritime communications between the Egyptians in the Red Sea, the Mesopotamians in the Persian Gulf and the Indus Valley civilization on the northwest coast of the Indian subcontinent had developed as early as the third millennium BCE (Possehl, 1982: 215–236; Tallet, 2016; Sidebotham, 2011). This maritime communication continued through the Sassanid dynasty and gained in importance during the Abbasid dynasty, when Basra (in modern-day southern Iraq) gained in importance as the international gateway to the capital at Baghdad (Whitehouse, 1985; Potts, 2009). By the tenth century, Middle Eastern ships were crossing back and forth between East Africa, the Arabian Sea and the west coast of the Indian subcontinent, as well as the Malay Peninsula and the South Chinese coast.

For the Indian subcontinent, maritime activities were already evident in the Bay of Bengal from the first millennium BCE onward. Tambralipti, for example, served as a port near the mouth of the Ganges River (Jahan, 2006; Tripati, 2017), while a number of wrecks, dated to the turn of the millennium, have been excavated near the river delta at Godavaya in south Sri Lanka, suggesting that a port city likely existed at that location (Gaur et al., 2011; Lawler, 2014). By the mid-first millennium CE, several ports had emerged along the east Indian coastline. These included Kanchipuram and Mahabalipuram. By the early eleventh century, the south Indians had developed shipping capabilities at a sufficiently high level that the Chola Kingdom was able to launch a naval expedition into the Melaka Straits (Kulke et al., 2009).

Cumulatively, all the major societies and regions of Maritime Asia were, by the mid-first millennium CE, in possession either of maritime gateways or nodal points that connected them to the rest of the maritime world or of maritime capacities that enabled their people to sail across the different zones of Maritime Asia. For Southeast Asia, this marked a departure from earlier periods. Whereas there has been little evidence of shipping networks from other regions traversing Southeast Asian waters prior to the mid-first millennium CE, by the second half of the first millennium CE, evidence from both texts and archaeology reflects a growing series of networks that traversed and serviced Southeast Asia. Southeast Asia's connection with the outside world was not dependent solely on its shipping capabilities but relied on other networks as well. These networks only intensified through the course of the late first through early second millennia CE.

Southeast Asian Shipping Networks

As a maritime zone, coastal Southeast Asia has seen, since prehistoric times, human migrations into and across the region by sea. Perhaps the earliest of these migrations were by Austronesians, emanating from south China, moving southward through coastal Mainland Southeast Asia and the Malay Peninsula, and into the east Indonesian archipelago and the Philippines (Bellwood, 1991). These sea-borne migratory experiences meant that, by the first millennium BCE, Maritime Southeast Asia had developed vessels that had large carrying capacities (Manguin, 2019).

In addition, given that Southeast Asia is primarily characterized as an archipelagic region, comprising thousands of islands that together form a tightly interconnected network of maritime landforms, the maritime zone has functioned not so much as a barrier to communication but rather as a conduit of exchange and interaction across Southeast Asia, linking coastal areas and riparian zones together and, by extension, the highland zones as well (Sopher 1977; Chou, 2012). The result has been that navigational technology and seafaring knowledge have been an integral aspect of Southeast Asia's culture for millennia. Maritime technology, essential for the successful navigation of riverine systems that enabled interaction between the highland, riparian and maritime zones, developed very early on in Southeast Asian history (Manguin, 2009).

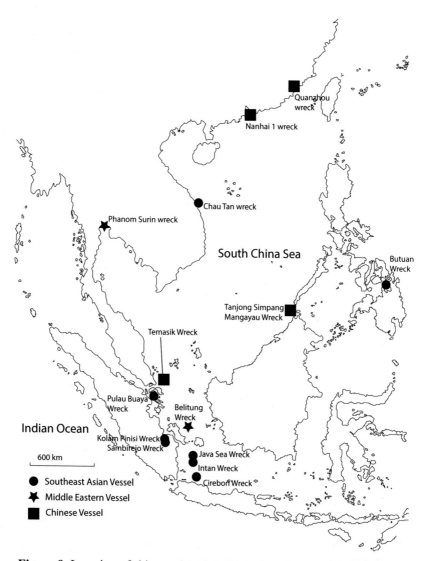

Figure 9 Location of shipwrecks in Maritime Southeast Asia and the South China Sea

Given the destructive environmental conditions of the tropics, physical evidence of riverine and maritime technology has, to date, appeared fairly late. The earliest known remains of an Indigenous vessel, excavated at Pontian, may be dated to the first century CE through ceramic typology and to the third through fifth centuries CE through radiocarbon dating of the ship's wooden remains (Ray, 1990; Manguin, 1996). Other remains include the Butuan wreck (Mindanao, c.third to fifth century CE), Kolam Pinisi wreck (Sumatra, c.fifth to seventh century CE) and Sambirejo wreck (Sumatra, c.seventh to eighth century CE) (Manguin, 1993: 258; McGrail, 2004: 298, 299). These are representative of Southeast Asia's riverine shipbuilding technology and demonstrate the ability of Southeast Asians to connect the coastal and delta regions to the inland areas through the river systems (ASEAN-COCI, 2006).

At the same time, vessels and geographical knowledge for the successful navigation of the seas and coasts of Southeast Asia also developed in tandem. One of the earliest pieces of evidence of such Southeast Asian ships comes from the Chau Tan wreck. Recovered off the coast of central Vietnam and dated to the late eighth century, the vessel appears to have been carrying a mixed cargo of Middle Eastern and Chinese ceramics when it foundered (Nishino et al., 2014). This indicates that Southeast Asian vessels had been serving as intraregional carriers through the first millennium CE.

This practice continued into the early second millennium CE. The Intan wreck, recovered near Belitung Island, has been dated to the late tenth century CE. The vessel was carrying a cargo of mixed origins, including Chinese ceramics, Chinese bronze mirrors, Chinese silver ingots, Chinese iron rods, Southeast Asian copper scrap, bronze architectural fittings and religious instruments, lead ingots, silver and tin, Southeast Asian food and natural products, such as candlenuts, ivory and benzoin, and Middle Eastern glass (Flecker, 2002: 62, 63). Chinese products, while clearly an important part of the ship's cargo, constituted a minority of what the ship was carrying.

A third wreck, dated to the late twelfth century, has been recovered in the Riau Archipelago. Named the Pulau Buaya wreck, the vessel was carrying a cargo of mixed origins, including Chinese ceramics, iron bars and woks, as well as a range of Southeast Asian products, including tin ingots, fine-paste earthenware *kendi*s (a type of Southeast Asian drinking vessel), copper ingots and other metal ingots. It appears to have been heading to a port in the west Java Sea, possibly along the southeast Sumatran or north Javanese coast, when it foundered (Ridho & McKinnon, 1998). It is possible that the vessel had begun its voyage from the South Chinese coast, although it is also likely that the Chinese cargo had been acquired at a port in the Gulf of Siam or on the Vietnamese coast, where its Southeast Asian cargo was also acquired.

These shipwrecks serve as a valuable source of information on Southeast Asia's global trade at the turn of the millennium. First, they illustrate the consistent pattern of demand for Chinese products by Southeast Asians from the eighth through twelfth centuries. These were primarily ceramics, ironware and lead ingots. Chinese silks are likely to have been another type of product that Southeast Asians acquired from China, although none have remained intact in the context of the shipwrecks. By the late twelfth century, precious metals do not appear to have been imported from China in any substantial quantities, although metals of cheaper value, or base metals that could be used in the production of alloys, were still in demand.

Additionally, at least up until the tenth century, Middle Eastern products, including ivory, glassware and ceramics, were in demand in Island Southeast Asia. By the twelfth century, perhaps with the decline in trade coming from the Middle East, products from that region of Maritime Asia appear to have disappeared from the Southeast Asian intraregional trade. In their place, Mainland Southeast Asian and Chinese products appear to have been desirable (Heng, 2013: 500).

A second, transregional Southeast Asian shipping network was also operating during the late first and early second millennia CE. These were ships that originated from Southeast Asia and connected the region with the other areas of Maritime Asia. The earliest example is the Cirebon wreck. Dated to the late ninth century, the wreck was recovered off the northeast coast of Java and was carrying a cargo of Chinese ironware and Chinese ceramics. The ship was also carrying several hundred kilograms of lapis lazuli. The only non-Chinese items were several Vajrayana Buddhist objects, which could have been the personal belongings of the ship's crew. This was therefore a Southeast Asian trading vessel that was returning from China to a port in Java when it foundered (Liebner, 2014: 178).

Another Southeast Asian vessel with similar characteristics is the Java Sea wreck. Recovered off Belitung Island in the west Java Sea, the vessel has been dated to the early thirteenth century and was carrying a cargo comprising Chinese ceramics and ironware (Figure 10). The only other items that were recovered from the wreck site were several pieces of Southeast Asian resin, possibly used as fire starters, sixteen elephant tusks, thirty-one Thai *kendi*s, two bronze figurines, a set of copper alloy weights and a few glass fragments. It is likely that these were the personal effects of the ship's crew (Mathers & Flecker, 1997: 191–197).

Figure 10 A stack of cast-iron cauldrons at the Java Sea wreck site, c. thirteenth
century
(Source: Pacific Sea Resources)

The Cirebon and Java Sea wrecks also share certain similar characteristics.
The first is their relative carrying capacities. The Cirebon wreck was carrying at
least 300 tons of cargo, while the Java Sea wreck appears to have had a capacity
of approximately 374 tons (Mathers & Flecker, 1997: 204). In contrast, the Intan
and Pulau Buaya wrecks both had capacities of only around 200 tons. In other
words, the Southeast Asian vessels used to ply the transregional trade were
significantly larger than those used for the intraregional trade. Taking all the
wrecks together, it would appear that Southeast Asian ships were operating
between south China and Island Southeast Asia, carrying cargo directly
between the two regions. Along with textual information from the Chinese
corpus, this suggests that such direct Southeast Asian shipping to China may
have taken place as early as the mid-first millennium CE.

By the fourteenth century, the transregional trade between China and
Southeast Asia appears to have been dominated by Chinese ships. The
Southeast Asian vessels of this period that have been recovered so far have
been those operating in the intraregional trade. These include the Nanyang
wreck, which was recovered off Tioman Island, along the east coast of
Peninsular Malaysia. The characteristics of this wreck were similar to those
from before the fourteenth century (Brown & Sjostrand, 2004: 46, 47).

Additionally, a different type of ship, known as the Southeast Asian hybrid vessel, was beginning to appear in the region. These vessels typically had the physical features of a Chinese ship, including compartmentalized hulls, but were constructed using Southeast Asian fastening techniques, such as the dowel-and-peg method. These vessels appeared in Southeast Asian waters only during the late fourteenth and fifteenth centuries, and it is not known where they primarily originated from. Nonetheless, the cargo of such wreck vessels, which comprised primarily Mainland Southeast Asian ceramics, suggests that these vessels likely operated from the ports of the Gulf of Siam and coastal Vietnam. These vessels may have arisen owing to the ban on private maritime activities imposed by the Ming court from 1371 to the mid-sixteenth century (Manguin 1993; Flecker, 2007). By the time the ban was lifted in 1567, European vessels, including those operated by the Portuguese, Spanish and Dutch, had entered the scene in Southeast Asia and south China, ushering in the early modern era.

Indian Shipping Networks

Indian shipping was operating in the Bay of Bengal as early as the first millennium BCE. Shipping and trade appear to have occurred along the west coast of the Indian subcontinent by the beginning of the first millennium CE. Wrecks have been located at such sites as the southern tip of Sri Lanka, including the Godavaya wreck, dated to the second century CE (Muthucumarana et al., 2014). The wreck data indicate that South Asian vessels from the Bay of Bengal littoral were sufficiently large to have been able to carry substantial amounts of cargo during this time. Such maritime capabilities would have enabled large-volume exchanges to have occurred between Southeast Asia and the east coast of the Indian subcontinent during this time.

Evidence for the development of shipping networks from the east Indian subcontinent to Southeast Asia may be found in the latter region as early as the late first millennium BCE. Sites along the east and west coasts of the Isthmus of Kra and the west coast of the Malay Peninsula have yielded substantial volumes of trade items that originated from the former region. These sites include Sungei Bujang, Khao Sam Kaeo, Ban Kluai Nok and Phu Khao Thong (Figure 11), and the material cultural remains recovered archaeologically include beads and earthenware ceramics, such as rouletted ware and black ware (Bellina-Pryce & Silapanth, 2006; Nik, 1994; Jacq-Hergoualc'h, 2002).

By the early first millennium CE, Buddhist temple structures and inscriptions began to appear at Sungei Bujang in South Kedah (Allen, 1988; Peacock, 1970; Quaritch-Wales & Quaritch-Wales, 1947). Inscriptions in Indic languages,

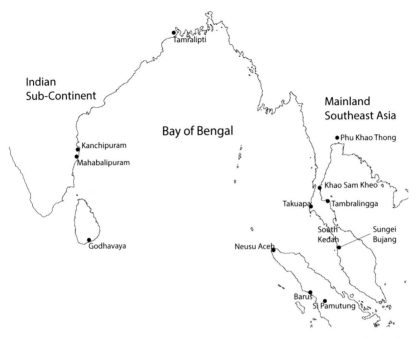

Figure 11 Port cities in the Bay of Bengal littoral and the Melaka Straits region related to Indian shipping and organized commercial networks

containing invocations of safe passage and arrival across the Bay of Bengal, have been recovered from this settlement site (Laidley, 1848). The content of the inscriptions suggests that the commissioners of the temples, the temple designs and the commemorative inscriptions were of Indian origin, as opposed to being local adaptations of Indic religious ideas in the first instance (Murphy, 2018). This suggests that Indian travelers, including merchants, rather than just Southeast Asian travelers, had been crossing the Bay of Bengal on a regular basis during the early first millennium CE, with the former frequently making landfall along the northwest Malay Peninsula coastline.

By the middle of the first millennium CE, more evidence for the regular passage of people and goods from the Indian subcontinent to Southeast Asia begins to emerge. Buddhist pilgrims, including those from China, have left a substantial number of records of their passage between China and South Asia, often making that passage via Southeast Asia (Sen, 2003: 63–112). One of these pilgrims, Fa Xian, traveling by sea from Sri Lanka back to China at the beginning of the fifth century, noted that the vessel he was on could carry up to 200 persons (Legge, 1886: 111). Yijing, who traveled to Nalanda in India via

Southeast Asia in the 670s and 680s, noted that both Southeast Asian and Indian ships were plying the route between the west Java Sea, the Straits of Melaka and the east Indian coastline (Takakusu, 1966).

At the same time, vestiges of Indic religious culture had begun to appear along the coast of Mainland Southeast Asia. In such areas as south-central Thailand and the Isthmus of Kra, remains of Buddhist architecture, as well as such small finds as clay votive tablets and statuettes, have been recovered from what have been termed Dvaravati urban sites (Lorrillard, 2014; Revire, 2014). Indic religious architecture and figurines have also been recovered along the coast of Mainland Southeast Asia, known at that time as the state of Champa (Lavy, 2003). Finally, Indic inscriptions have been recovered from Kutai (Borneo) and Palembang (Sumatra) (Figure 12), to name but a few examples (Sarip, 2020; Kulke, 1993). The absence of widespread adoption of Indic religious cultural traits, such as decorative elements, lexicon and iconography, suggests that these are indicative of the presence of South Asians, likely bringing with them vestiges of their cultures as they traveled to Southeast Asia. It is likely that these voyages were conducted using South Asian vessels, even as Southeast Asian vessels were also involved.

Figure 12 (Left) Yupa inscription, fifth century CE, from Kutai, Muara Kaman, Kalimantan, Indonesia (Source: Wikimedia Commons: https://commons .wikimedia.org/wiki/File:153_Mulavarman_Inscription,_Muara_Kaman,_ Kalimantan,_5th_c_(23406879131).jpg)
(Right) Telegu Batu inscription, 683 CE, Palembang, South Sumatra, Indonesia (Source: Wikimedia Commons: https://commons.wikimedia.org/wiki/File:Telaga_ Batu_inscription.JPG)

By the tenth century, records of Indian sojourners began to appear in Central Java, in the vicinity of the Prambanan Plain. By the fourteenth century, such evidence extended to north Sumatra at Padang Lawas (Christie, 1998). These were inscriptions recorded in Tamil, the language of the south Indian kingdom of Chola. Indeed, the capabilities of South Asian shipping across the Bay of Bengal appear to have reached a new height in the early eleventh century, when the Chola Kingdom launched a naval expedition into the Straits of Melaka. The expedition, which led to the capture of the ruler of Srivijaya and his extradition to India, as well as the sacking of port cities in the Melaka Straits, appears to have been precipitated by the Chola's desire to establish its supremacy over the commercial centers of the Straits region (Meenakshisundararajan, 2009). The existence of a vibrant shipping network emanating from the Chola kingdom would have to have been a necessary precondition for such an expedition to have been a worthwhile endeavor. Indeed, the vibrant operations of Tamil maritime networks, including a number of trade guilds (Hall 1978 & 2006), as evidenced by an eleventh century Tamil inscription recovered from Barus (northwest Sumatra), the profusion of south Indian ceramics at such sites as Kota Cina in northeast Sumatra (McKinnon, 1977), and the profusion of Hindu temple sites at Sungei Bujang and Sungei Muda (South Kedah) with layouts emulating the temples of coastal south India, would suggest that this was likely the case during the eleventh through thirteenth centuries.

The Indian shipping networks appear to have declined by the fourteenth century. The extent of Indian architectural, material-cultural and epigraphic remains that characterized the Melaka Straits and Java dwindled and disappeared through the fourteenth century. This was likely due to the changes in geopolitics on the Indian subcontinent itself. By the second half of the thirteenth century, the Chola Kingdom had come to an end. In its place, the ascendant kingdoms in south and central India, including Vijayanagar, adopted a more insular outlook than their predecessors. The result may have been that Indian shipping networks, which had flourished under state patronage from the second half of the first millennium through to the early second millennium CE, began to recede in the face of other networks that were operating in Southeast Asia by the fourteenth century.

Middle Eastern Shipping Networks

Through the course of the first millennium CE, the rise of powerful states in the Middle East – the Sassanid Kingdom in the third to the seventh century, the Umayyad Caliphate in the seventh to eleventh centuries and the Abbasid Caliphate in the eighth to the thirteenth century – provided the political and economic energy for the expansion of Middle Eastern seaborne trade out of the Arabian Sea into the west Indian Ocean.

While shipping and maritime technology had already been developed in the west Indian Ocean as early as the third millennium BCE, it was in the mid-first millennium CE, following the expansion of these Middle Eastern states and the rise of relations with proximate first-tier states such as those in the Indian subcontinent, Europe, North Africa and China, that Middle Eastern shipping extended its networks beyond the west Indian Ocean into the Bay of Bengal, the Java Sea and the South China Sea. Siraf in the second century CE, followed by Basra in the eighth century and Hormuz by the early second millennium CE, served as international gateways of the Middle East into Maritime Asia (Averbuch, 2013; Khakzad, 2012; Lamb, 1964). The Abbasid Caliphate in particular, with its capital located at Baghdad, provided the demand for international products that propelled Middle Eastern trade across Maritime Asia to new heights.

Southeast Asia had become increasingly familiar to Middle Eastern geographers through the second half of the first millennium CE. Given the fact that any passage from the Arabian Sea to south China would have taken one year due to the monsoon patterns and the direction of sail, it would have been likely that Middle Easterners would have sojourned at the port cities of Southeast Asia to facilitate the passage of Middle Eastern vessels and merchants along the Arabian Sea to south China route. In addition, the shifts in geopolitics in the Middle East also had the effect of dispersing Middle Easterners across the Asian continent. The collapse of the Sassanid Kingdom in 650 CE led to the migration of Persian elites to such nearby places as the west coast of the Indian subcontinent, and as far east as the Chinese city of Yangzhou, located just slightly upriver from the Yangzi delta. Additionally, at Guangzhou, a substantial Middle Eastern community had established itself by the Tang dynasty. Consequently, Middle Eastern geographical treatises of the period by such authors as Ibn Khordadbeh (mid-ninth century), Abu Zaid (early tenth century) and Al-Masudi (mid-tenth century) mention such places as Barus, Kedah, Srivijaya Palembang, Java, Khmer Cambodia and Champa along the passage to south China (Tibbetts, 1979: 27–39). Between the eleventh and fourteenth centuries, the same phenomenon was occurring at Quanzhou, which suggests that similar sojourning experiences were occurring in Southeast Asia as well, this time at such places as Lambri, Semudra-Pasai, Srivijaya-Jambi, Java, Borneo and Champa (Tibbetts, 1979: 57–65).

Evidence for Middle Eastern shipping across Southeast Asia during global premodernity comes by way of two wrecks that have been excavated in

Southeast Asian waters. The first is the Phanom Surin wreck. Located in the first millennium CE coastline of the Gulf of Thailand, south of modern-day Bangkok, this Middle Eastern wreck has been dated to the early ninth century (Guy, 2017). A second wreck – the Belitung wreck (Figure 13) – was recovered in the west Java Sea near Belitung Island, and has been dated to the 820s to 840s (Krahl 2010; Chong, Murphy & Flecker, 2017; Flecker 2000 & 2001; G. Heng 2019). These remain the only Middle Eastern shipwrecks to be identified in the region, and suggest that the height of Middle Eastern shipping networks across Southeast Asia may have been in the ninth century.

The cargo of the wrecks provides some sense of the nature of Middle Eastern shipping activities in Southeast Asia. The Phanom Surin wreck, whose hold was almost devoid of any commercial cargo except for several Middle Eastern torpedo jars (jars with pointed bottoms, resembling an amphora in form), suggests that the vessel had unloaded its original cargo and was likely going to be laden with products that could be sourced in the Gulf of Siam littoral when it sank. It would appear that the vessel was operating between the Middle East and Southeast Asia due to the presence of the Middle Eastern ceramic containers (Guy, 2017: 186).

The Belitung wreck's cargo, on the other hand, illustrates a different shipping network. The vessel was carrying a cargo that almost was entirely composed of Chinese items, including a large quantity of Chinese ceramics, silver ingots, several storage jars containing star anise, lead ingots, silverware and several pieces of goldware (Chong et al., 2017: 12). The absence of Southeast Asian products in the cargo hold, and the predominantly Chinese cargo that the vessel was carrying, suggest that it was heading for the Indian Ocean when it foundered. In other words, the vessel was likely operating as part of a transoceanic network that connected the Middle East directly with China (Heng, 2017: 148).

It would appear, therefore, that two networks were operated by Middle Eastern ships in the ninth century: a sectoral network that connected the Middle East with the Indian Ocean and Southeast Asia, and a transoceanic network that connected the Middle East directly with south China.

Shipping networks that originated in the Middle East, as evidenced by wrecks that were constructed primarily of materials that originated from the west Indian Ocean, appear to have been active up until the end of the first millennium CE. From the early second millennium CE onwards, such vessels no longer appear to have been present in Southeast Asia in substantial numbers. Instead, we have textual records of Middle Eastern sojourners, both in Southeast Asia and south China, beginning to outfit vessels at these locations and operating shipping networks from the port cities of these places. These included such well-known Middle Eastern personalities as Pu Shougeng (1250–1281), who was resident in

Figure 13 A model of the Jewel of Muscat, a dhow built in Qantab, Oman, between 2008 and 2010, modeled after the Belitung wreck (Source: Wikimedia Commons: https://commons.wikimedia.org/wiki/File:Jewel_of_Muscat,_ Maritime_Experiential_Museum_%26_Aquarium,_Singapore_-_20120102– 02.jpg)

Quanzhou, served as the superintendent of mercantile shipping at that port city during the Yuan period and was known to have owned one of the largest fleets of trading vessels at the port city (Kuwabara, 1928; Luo, 1955).

Chinese Shipping Networks

As a landmass with a number of major riverine systems, including the Yellow River and Yangzi River, China's inhabitants have been utilizing these systems for mass transportation since the end of the first millennium BCE. Specific to south China, the depth of the Yangzi River enabled vessels with deeper hulls to operate. Additionally, travel along the Chinese coastline occurred for much of the period, particularly along the south Chinese coast over which the monsoons blew. Consequently, coastal craft were developed in south China, even though these vessels did not possess the rudders needed for open-sea sailing (Deng & Kang, 1997; Deng, 1999).

While south China, with its port cities at Guangzhou, Jiankang, Yangzhou and Hangzhou (Figure 14), had been receiving foreign vessels arriving via the South China Sea since the Han dynasty, China itself does not appear to have developed any shipping networks into Maritime Asia. This is not to say that the Chinese did not venture into Southeast Asia or the Indian Ocean. As early as the third century CE, for example, the Eastern Wu Dynasty in south China had sent an embassy to Funan in the Gulf of Siam (Manguin, 2014). The Chinese diplomats subsequently brought back intelligence on the Southeast Asian state and its neighboring areas, as well as the Indian subcontinent and Middle East. The most important textual information they provided was on the Gulf of Siam (Wheatley, 1961: 14). By the mid-first millennium CE, Chinese Buddhist pilgrims were traveling to and from the Indian subcontinent by sea. Chinese vessels, however, were not mentioned in any of these records. Additionally, no shipwreck of Chinese origin datable to the first millennium CE has been discovered. In other words, there is almost no trace of Chinese ships operating in Southeast Asia prior to the tenth century.

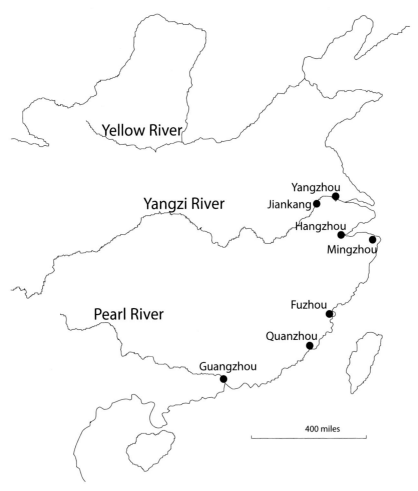

Figure 14 Location of international ports in China during the Global Middle
Ages

It is only in the tenth century that references to Chinese shipping into Southeast Asia begin to appear. Song period official texts of the tenth and eleventh centuries mention Chinese ships heading from South Chinese ports down to Southeast Asia, even though this activity was not encouraged by the Song court. As an example, poems from south China, including Fujian Province, mention the draw of the sea for the coastal people of this area as a source of economic activity (So, 2000: 23). Additionally, the *Pingzhou ketan* (c.1117), which contains detailed descriptions of the commercial activities at Guangzhou, notes that Chinese ships had been sailing to Southeast Asia for some time. The text notes that vessels from the South Chinese coast had to report to the ports of Guangzhou, Mingzhou or Hangzhou to register their trip before they could leave for Southeast Asia, and the additional time involved in this administrative procedure resulted in an extended sailing time which also impacted the cost of shipping (Heng, 2006: 8–18).

By the late eleventh century, the rules pertaining to Chinese shipping were liberalized by the Song court. Chinese vessels were now permitted to freely leave from any port as long as their departure was registered with a local administrative office. Ships were permitted to remain abroad for nine months. Any vessel that violated the rule would be fined and have their cargo confiscated. This rule appears to have been in place up through to the end of the Song dynasty in 1278 (Heng, 2012: 42–44). The fact that the rule included punitive measures of enforcement that were commercial in nature indicates that it was Chinese commercial shipping that was being addressed here.

The length of time permitted for each sailing voyage had the effect of compelling Chinese shipping networks to focus on an immediate neighboring region that could be reached in one cycle of monsoon as the area of operations. For Chinese shipping heading south, Southeast Asia became the key area of commercial operations, as vessels could depart from November to January with the northeast monsoon, and return with the southwest monsoon from April to August (Heng, 2017). Consequently, Chinese knowledge of Southeast Asia, particularly commercial, navigational, political and even anthropological and cultural knowledge of the region's people, grew through the course of the late eleventh through fourteenth centuries.

It is in this context that we should see the wrecks of Chinese origin that have been recovered in Southeast Asia. The earliest of these wrecks is the Tanjong Simpang Mangayau wreck (Baszley, Basrah & Bala, 2009). Dated to the late tenth century and discovered off the coast of north Sabah (East Malaysia), the vessel was carrying a large cargo of Chinese ceramics as well as a small amount of bronze items. The wreck's location and the cargo suggest that Chinese shipping networks had begun to extend to the ports on the north coast of Borneo Island by the end of the tenth century.

A second wreck – the Nanhai 1 wreck – was discovered off the Chinese coast near the Pearl River delta in Guangdong Province. Dated to the late twelfth to early thirteenth century, the Chinese vessel was carrying a cargo of predominantly south Fujian ceramics, along with a smaller quantity of storage jars. The wreck was also carrying silver ingots, Chinese coins and several gold items (Nanhai No. 1, 2018: 2). The vessel appears to have been on its way to Southeast Asia, most likely having departed from the port city of Quanzhou or a port along the south Fujian coast, when it foundered.

Finally, a third wreck – the Quanzhou wreck – was discovered in an inlet bay of Quanzhou Harbor in Fujian Province, which has silted over in modern times (Figure 15). Dated to the 1270s, the vessel had returned to China and was carrying a cargo of Southeast Asian products, including pepper, gharuwood, sandalwood, betel nuts and cinnabar, when it foundered. The cargo being intact in the wreck's hull, it would appear that the vessel was intentionally scuttled after it had come into port, likely due to the unstable situation in south Fujian in the face of Mongol forces advancing along the South Chinese coastline (Merwin, 1977: 18–51).

Taken together, the three wrecks provide insights into several characteristics of Chinese shipping networks operating into Southeast Asia. First, the vessels that operated in Southeast Asia had substantial carrying capacities. The Nanhai 1 wreck had an approximate capacity of three hundred and forty tons. The Quanzhou wreck had a capacity of around three hundred tons. This meant that

Figure 15 Excavation of the Quanzhou wreck, 1974, at Houtu Harbor, Fujian Province (Source: UNESCO Silk Roads Program: https://en.unesco.org/silkroad/content/quanzhou#pid=8)

Chinese vessels were able to carry a lot of cargo between points across the South China Sea. As a comparison, the Middle Eastern wrecks – Phanom Surin and Belitung – had capacities of approximately half of these Chinese vessels.

Secondly, Chinese shipping connected the hinterlands of the Chinese coastal ports to Southeast Asia in a direct manner. The economic output of the South Chinese coastal hinterland, including ceramics and iron, became the key products that were exported to Southeast Asia in large volumes. Thirdly, Chinese shipping networks appear to have focused on specific areas of Southeast Asia and specialized in imported products that were available from these specific places.

By the advent of Yuan dynastic rule in south China in 1279, Chinese shipping in Southeast Asia had become highly developed. While there were initial restrictions imposed on Chinese merchants operating in Southeast Asia, these restrictions were lifted by the 1320s, enabling Chinese shipping networks not only to resume operations in Southeast Asia but also to extend further westward into the Bay of Bengal (Heng, 2012: 42–44; Schurmann, 1967). By the mid-fourteenth century, Chinese shipping was such an important means of travel between the Bay of Bengal and China that such travelers as Ibn Battuta, seeking passage from the Indian subcontinent to Southeast Asia and China, noted that all travel across the Bay of Bengal and Southeast Asia was undertaken on Chinese ships (Bivar, 2000). Chinese shippers were so familiar with Southeast Asian and Bay of Bengal waters that, at the end of the fourteenth century, with the advent of Ming rule in China and the subsequent maritime ban that was imposed on Chinese shipping by the Ming court, Chinese shipping networks were able to relocate in Southeast Asia and continue their commercial activities in Maritime Asia from there.

Shipping Networks and Southeast Asia's Interaction with the Global World of Premodernity

Through the course of the late first to early second millennium CE, shipping networks from the Middle East, the Indian subcontinent and China operated in Southeast Asian waters in different periods. These networks provided the shipping capabilities that facilitated Southeast Asia's interaction across Maritime Asia, at a time when global commerce and economic production were on the increase. These networks enabled the region to develop not only its transregional interactions but also intraregional exchanges between Mainland and Island Southeast Asia.

These networks did not all operate concurrently. Specific networks would dominate certain periods of time, all the while complementing the Southeast

Asian shipping networks that were already operating as early as the first millennium CE. The ebbs and flows of these various networks reflected the merchant networks that operated in Southeast Asia, which Section 4 addresses.

4 Merchant Networks across Southeast Asia

Shipping networks across Southeast Asia were supported in the premodern period by a series of organized merchant networks emanating from the various regions of Maritime Asia. These networks served a number of important functions. They allowed for representation and agency to be established at the various port cities along the maritime trade routes. These agencies served as the land-based originating and receiving nodes of the shipping networks, facilitating the flow of products and people from one port to another (Abu-Lughod, 1989; Hall, 2009).

The agencies also facilitated the procurement of items produced in the economic hinterlands of the port cities. These included products for which these places were known. The Chinese ports of Guangzhou, Hangzhou, Yangzhou and Quanzhou, for example, exported high-fired stoneware, silks, metalware and foodstuffs (Huang, 2003). The ports of the Indian subcontinent, such as Mahabalipuram and Kanchipuram (Gaur, 2011; Ray 1989; Verma 2005), were known for the export of pepper, cotton textiles, earthenware ceramics and their contents, and precious stones. The merchant networks operating at the port cities were able to order, collate and ship these products across Maritime Asia in an effective and reliable manner, thereby establishing consistent supplies of such products, and capitalizing on the annual rhythm of shipping across Maritime Asia for large-scale transportation of these trade items.

Agents at foreign port cities, where products were being received from their respective places of origin, also allowed for demand for the imported goods to be tested, cultivated and possibly even secured prior to the arrival of the ships and their cargo. In this regard, these agents would have helped to facilitate the establishment of a predictable demand at the receiving market, thereby enabling the minimization of risk related to transregional trade through the establishment of market predictability in long-distance trade and the reducing of the absence of information on a foreign market. Each of the regions of Maritime Asia had their respective organized networks. Southeast Asia, in the nexus of Maritime Asia, became a beneficiary of the presence of these networks.

Indian Guilds

Perhaps the earliest non-Southeast Asian commercial networks to operate in the region were the Indian guilds of the first and early second millennia CE. These guilds were established through the granting of commercial charters by the states that served as their patrons. These included the Pandyan and Chola Kingdoms (Abraham, 1988; Hall, 1978 & 2003; Karashima, 2009). The guilds served as the economic lifeblood of the premodern South Asian economy, connecting the economic output of the rural hinterlands of these kingdoms with the land and seaborne trade of the Indian subcontinent. These networks in turn extended abroad to include Southeast Asia, China, the Middle East and East Africa (Subbarayalu, 2009).

In Southeast Asia, these guilds operated along the coast and in the upland areas of north Sumatra, the east and west coasts of the Isthmus of Kra and the north Malay Peninsula, and Java (Christie, 1998; Guy, 2012). Despite the apparent importance of these guilds in the region's commerce, relatively little is known of how they operated at the Southeast Asian port cities where they evidently established a presence. Much of what is known has been deduced from the small cache of epigraphic records, as well as the architectural remains, that speak of their activities in the region.

One of the earliest pieces of evidence of Indian commercial activities and presence in Southeast Asia may be found at the Sungei Bujang area in South Kedah. Built between the fifth and tenth centuries, the temple bases at this location are reminiscent of the architectural layout of temples of the same period located along the east Indian coast at such places as Mahabalipuram and Kanchipuram (Figure 16). As opposed to an adoption and adaptation of Indian architectural elements, as may be seen in Javanese religious architecture of the eighth and ninth centuries, it would appear that the communities that commissioned the construction of these temples in South Kedah were replicating religious architecture on the other side of the Bay of Bengal.

Indeed, the inscriptions of this period recovered from South Kedah invoke the blessings of the deities that the temples have been dedicated to, seeking safe passage across the Bay of Bengal (Figure 17). An inscription, recovered at Takuapa on the west coast of the Isthmus of Kra and dated to the ninth century, contains the record of the construction of a tank, typically used for ceremonial washing by Hindus, and the transfer of its custodianship to the *Manigramam*, a Tamil merchant guild (Sastri, 1949; Wade, 2009: 236). Taken together, these inscriptions and architectural remains show that Indian organized commercial networks were entrenched at the north Melaka Straits region by the late first millennium CE, with a significant community sojourning in this area to require the construction of such religious features.

By the late eleventh century, it would appear that Indian merchant networks had established their presence in north Sumatra as well. A Tamil inscription dated to 1088, recovered at Lobu Tua (Barus), records instructions for the

Figure 16 Candi Batu Pahat (Hindu temple base), South Kedah, Malaysia
(c.sixth century AD) (Source: Wikimedia Commons: https://commons
.wikimedia.org/wiki/File:Candi_Batu_Pahat_of_Bujang_Valley.jpg)

collection of a levy on commercial vessels that was imposed by a guild that was
called the *Disai ayirattu ainnurruvar* (Five Hundred of the Thousand
Directions) (Christie 1998: 257–258). Another inscription, dated to the twelfth
century and recovered from Neusu Aceh, mentions the existence of rules
pertaining to the collection of interest and the transaction of commercial
products (Christie 1998: 259). Finally, thirteenth-century inscriptions containing Indian script have been recovered from the east coast of the Isthmus of Kra.

Taken together, it would appear that Indian organized commercial networks
were able to establish agency presence and sojourning communities at a number
of locations in Island Southeast Asia during the fifth through fourteenth centuries. The location of the Tamil inscriptions and Tamil religious architecture
suggests that, at least in terms of the Tamil merchant networks and guilds,
north Sumatra, the Isthmus of Kra and the north Malay Peninsula formed

Figure 17 Rubbing of the Mahanavika Buddhagupta stone inscription, fifth century CE, found in Penang, Malaysia (Source: Wikimedia Commons: https://commons.wikimedia.org/wiki/File:Mahanavika_Buddhagupta_stone_inscription,_5th_century_CE,_Indian_Museum,_Kolkota.jpg)

a nexus in Maritime Southeast Asia where these organizations were able to establish themselves, serving as the area of call for Indian shipping and traders operating across the Bay of Bengal and further afield into south China.

By the fourteenth century, the Indian networks began to recede. On the Indian subcontinent, the shift in geopolitics inland, and the subsequent rise of Vijayanagar and the supplanting of the Cholas, led to the decline of these guilds in terms of their international reach (Wade, 2019). State support, which had enabled the establishment of commercial activities over great distances in the first instance, became a prime factor in the decline of those networks when support was ultimately withdrawn.

Middle Eastern Networks

Middle Eastern organized commercial networks in Maritime Asia were premised on the logic of connecting the two terminus markets of the Middle East at the one end and China at the other. This long-distance interaction appears to have been in operation by the mid-first millennium CE, initiated by the Sassanid Dynasty (Wolters, 1967; Wade, 2009: 231–235). By the eighth century, following the installation of the Abbasid Caliphate capital at Baghdad and the resulting prominence of the port city of Basra on the Persian Gulf, two Middle Eastern networks emerged (Wink, 1990: 65; 1997: 1; Chaffee, 2018). The first was Persian, which succeeded the Sassanid Dynasty's network. Persian refugees, leaving the Sassanid Kingdom after its fall, began to move eastward across Asia, establishing sojourning communities in such places in China as Chang'an, Yangzhou (on the Yangzi delta) and Guangzhou (on the Pearl River Delta), and on the northwest coast of the Indian subcontinent (Heng, 2017; Schottenhammer, 2016). These sojourning Persian communities were established to facilitate the long-distance trade between the west Indian Ocean and China. There is little evidence to suggest that sojourning Persian communities were established in Southeast Asia during this time. The Belitung wreck, which likely called at Yangzhou some time in the early ninth century, and was carrying a cargo primarily sourced from the economic hinterland of the east Yangzi region just upstream of Yangzhou and heading toward the Indian Ocean when it foundered, likely exemplified this long-distance trade (Heng, 2017).

The second network was the Arab network. This network likely arose by the seventh century, originating in the Persian Gulf and Red Sea, and terminating at Guangzhou, where a substantial Arab sojourning community took root. This network was able to be mobile, suggesting that it was supported by a shipping network that it controlled. Its level of mobility and overall capability were sufficiently high that, in 758, this community was able to sack the city of Guangzhou, as a response to its unhappiness with the conditions imposed upon it by the officials there, and was able to abandon the port city and relocate elsewhere in Southeast Asia (Heng, 2017: 149, 152). Its mobility suggests that the Arab network was likely operating between China and Southeast Asia, and not just in the long-distance trade between China and the Middle East.

The Arab network continued to develop well into the early second millennium CE. The port cities of Guangzhou and Quanzhou, which were the key Chinese ports that engaged in economic interactions with Southeast Asia, were hosts to substantial Arab communities during the tenth through fourteenth centuries. The Arabs were allowed to maintain cemeteries and to build mosques, including the Qingjing Mosque at Quanzhou (Figure 18) (established in 1009). A small number, who had been accorded titles by the Song court, were also permitted to travel beyond the port city's boundaries to engage in trade within China (Heng, 2012: 118).

The vast majority, however, could only engage in commerce at the port city. As such, this Middle Eastern network also likely operated between China and the Middle East, with Southeast Asia as the convergence zone, as well as within Southeast Asia as a regional network. The ninth-century Phanom Surin wreck, a Middle Eastern wreck that exhibited repairs using Island Southeast Asian shipbuilding techniques and which contained no cargo other than a small quantity of elephant tusks and several empty amphorae of Middle Eastern origin, suggests that this Arab network was operating commercially between Mainland and Island Southeast Asia for

Figure 18 Qingjing Mosque, located at Quanzhou, Fujian, China (Source: Wikimedia Commons: https://commons.wikimedia.org/wiki/File:Quanzhou_ Qingjing_Si_20120229-03.jpg)

substantial periods of time (Guy, 2017: 179–196). It was also during this time that individuals with Muslim names began to appear in Chinese records in Mainland Southeast Asia, including Champa, Vietnam and Java (Wade, 2010). This Arab network in Southeast Asia and China continued into the fourteenth century. Sojourners of Arab descent had by this time gained so much in status that, under the Ortaq policy of the Yuan Dynasty, individuals such as Pu Shougeng were able not only to own fleets of merchant vessels that operated between the two regions but also to be key players in the administration of the trade in China (Masaki, 2010; Kuwabara, 1928).

Chinese Networks

Among the Maritime Asian networks in Southeast Asia, Chinese networks were one of the later ones to operate in the region. Through the course of the first millennium CE, the administrative rules of the dynasties that were centered in the central Chinese plains, such as the Han, Sui and Tang Dynasties, did not permit Chinese vessels to go abroad to engage in trade. Instead, China relied on foreign shipping and merchants arriving annually at its coastal port cities, via the monsoon winds, to bring the products that it desired and consumed (Heng 2012: 48–50). In turn, Chinese products were exported to the rest of the global economy via these foreign networks. China's role in its maritime trade with Southeast Asia and the Indian Ocean littoral was therefore as a passive recipient. Nor were Chinese individuals allowed to travel abroad. The surviving records in the Chinese corpus show that travel to Southeast Asia by Chinese individuals, such as the envoys Zhu Ying and Kan Tai, representing the Eastern Wu Dynasty, and Buddhist pilgrims such as Yi Xing and Fa Xian, were either state-sponsored missions or had to be permitted by the state. Commerce and the establishment of networks at Southeast Asian port cities and economic centers were not the prime objectives of these missions.

Given the proximity of the Vietnamese coastline to south China, it is not surprising that as early as the first century BCE, the Chinese state, whenever it was consolidated and assertive in south China, would establish military commanderies or administrative districts in the Red River delta. These administrative systems included personnel who were responsible for the commerce that was conducted at these places (Brindley, 2021). Less clear were the policies and perspectives of the kingdoms that variously governed over south China during the interregnum period from the collapse of the Han dynasty to the advent of Tang rule (third to seventh century CE). The southward and maritime orientation of southeast China would have naturally predisposed the Chinese here not only to engage Southeast Asians along the south Chinese coast, but also to reach out to at least the northern coast of Mainland Southeast Asia. The commercial centers of the Red River delta in north Vietnam (historically known as Jiaozhi to the Chinese), as well as the port cities along the central Vietnamese coast (historically known as Champa to the Chinese), would have been accessible by coastal craft and easily disposed to cabotage trade (Shiro, 1998; Li, 2006; Cooke, Li & Anderson, 2011). While some trade likely did occur, the absence of coherent state policies supporting maritime trade resulted in a general dearth of records of Chinese commercial activities in Southeast Asia through most of the first millennium CE.

Conversely, Island Southeast Asia, as well as the Isthmus of Kra and the Malay Peninsula, would have required open-sea sailing to get to and from south China. The setup needed by Chinese commercial interests to operate in these parts of Southeast Asia, such as the shipping networks and agencies established at key Southeast Asian ports, would have had to have been similar to those of organized commercial networks originating from other parts of Maritime Asia, such as the Middle East and South Asia. It was not until the late eleventh century that such organized Chinese networks began to appear in Southeast Asia. For much of the first millennium CE, with the exception of the tenth century Tanjong Simpang Mangayau wreck, no evidence has shown that a Chinese shipping network was operating in the region until the twelfth century.

In 1072, as part of the Wang Anshi reforms, the Song court instituted a number of fiscal reforms that impacted China's international maritime trade (Drechsler, 2013; Williamson, 1935). Chinese ships were permitted, for the first time in history, to sail abroad from any port, as long as the trip was registered. Ships were allowed to be abroad for up to nine months, while Chinese individuals could stay abroad indefinitely. These policy changes allowed Chinese shipping to operate effectively in the areas which vessels leaving south China's coast could reach and return from within one monsoon cycle (i.e. nine months). This included Island Southeast Asia (Heng, 2012: 52, 53).

Additionally, import duties and compulsory purchases were adjusted over the course of the eleventh century, and reached their lowest levels during the reforms period, while the number of foreign products designated as state monopoly items were progressively reduced to only eight – rhinoceros horns, ivory, frankincense, tortoise shells, turtle carapaces, steel, coral and agate. This policy had the effect of spurring the import trade in foreign products, as Chinese traders were now able to meet market demand directly and match consumer tastes and need with the supply of products from abroad, especially Southeast Asia (Heng, 2013).

Taken together, these policy changes invigorated Chinese commercial activities in Southeast Asia. The volume of Chinese products exported to Southeast Asia increased substantially, reflecting the convergence of the economic output of the Chinese coastal hinterland with the Chinese export trade to the region. Whereas previously, the Chinese ceramics that made their way to Southeast Asia were sourced from such inland ceramic districts as Changsha, Ding and Gongxian, the range of Chinese ceramics that began to be made available in Southeast Asia from the late eleventh century were sourced primarily from those in the South Chinese coastal provinces, such as Nanhai, Jinjiang and Meixian in Guangdong Province, Cizao, Dehua, Quanzhou and Jian in Fujian Province, Longquan in Zhejiang Province and Jingdezhen in Jiangxi Province (Figure 19) (Ho, 2001; Heng, 2013: 496, 497). The Yue wares of Zhejiang Province appear to have been the only exception, having already been exported to Southeast Asia in fairly large quantities from the late first millennium CE onwards.

Chinese textual records of Southeast Asian port cities and states, in particular those involved heavily in international trade, began to contain increasingly detailed economic and commercial information from the mid-twelfth century onwards. The *Lingwai daida* (c.1178), for example, is one of the earliest Chinese texts to contain detailed commercial information of the key trading states of Southeast Asia, including Champa, north Vietnam, Srivijaya-Jambi, Palembang, Java, Borneo and Myanmar (Zhou & Tu, 1996: 29–47). By the early thirteenth century, texts such as the *Zhufanzhi* (c.1225; written by Zhao Rugua, the Superintendent for Mercantile Shipping at Quanzhou), record commercial information concerning a larger number of states and port polities in Southeast Asia, with a notable expansion in the number of port polities located in Island Southeast Asia, in particular the Melaka Straits and the west Java Sea littoral (Chen & Qian, 2000; Hirth & Rockhill, 1970). Finally, by the mid-fourteenth century, texts such as the *Daoyi zhilue* (c.1349; written by Wang Dayuan, who was traveling in Southeast Asia in the 1320s and 1330s) contain commercial information on as many as twenty ports in the Melaka Straits alone (Heng, 2012: 106). Additionally, through the late twelfth to mid-fourteenth century, the information on goods exported from the ports, as noted in the texts, as well as the products demanded by the markets that these ports serviced, grew in range and detail.

This growth of information in the Chinese textual corpus suggests that, from the late twelfth century onwards, organized Chinese commercial networks had made sufficient inroads into Southeast Asia such that detailed information needed for consistent commercial exchanges between China and Southeast Asia could be accrued. However, there is relatively little information as to whether Chinese traders were taking root in Southeast Asia and establishing sojourning communities

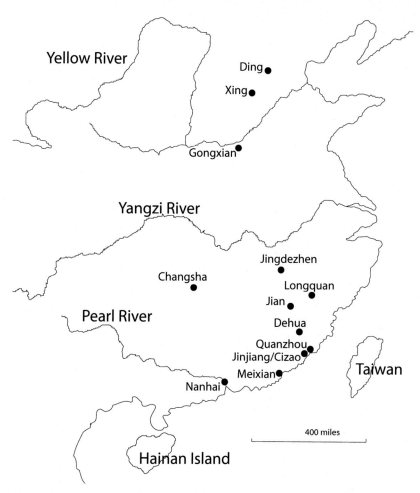

Figure 19 Location of Chinese kiln districts that produced ceramics exported to Southeast Asia

at the region's port cities in the organized and institutional way that South Asian and Middle Eastern traders were doing in the mid-first to early second millennium CE. The few Chinese texts that provide such information are relatively brief on the issue. The *Pingzhou ketan* (c.1116; written by Zhu Yu), for example, which contains eyewitness accounts and secondhand information of the trade-related activities at the port city of Guangzhou, notes that, by the early twelfth century, Chinese merchants were known to have sojourned abroad for as long as ten years. Merchants would rent cargo spaces on vessels by the foot, and would fill them with Chinese products such as ceramics, silks and metalware. Southeast Asian and Indian Ocean littoral products were made available at Southeast Asian ports in return (Heng, 2006: 14–15). From the presence of agents' tallies in the Quanzhou

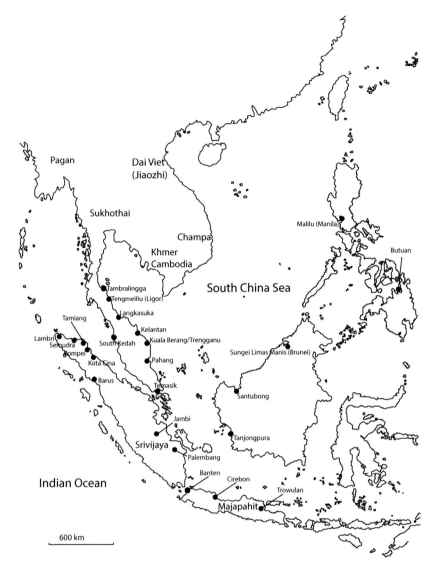

Figure 20 Southeast Asian port cities and kingdoms, as noted in the *Daoyi Zhilue* (c.1349)

wreck, which was returning to the port of Quanzhou when it foundered, it would appear that merchants were relying on agents who would effect the commercial transactions in Southeast Asia on their behalf (Merwin, 1977: 25; Heng, 2008: 38).

In other words, knowledge of Southeast Asia, and the frequency and ease with which Chinese agents could travel to the region in relatively short periods of time, were high enough that there may not have been a need for agents to be sojourning in Southeast Asian ports. Indeed, the shift from having knowledge of the commercial activities and market characteristics of a few key Southeast Asian ports, as reflected by the information in texts dated to the late twelfth century, to having similar degrees of knowledge of a large number of ports in the region, as reflected by texts of the mid-fourteenth century, suggests that Chinese traders' activities grew increasingly dispersed across Southeast Asia, involving not just the major entrepôt ports but also the minor ones, in almost all parts of Southeast Asia (Figure 20).

One of the ways in which increased familiarity with Southeast Asia was reflected in Chinese texts was the social characteristics of the locals of which the Chinese who were traveling in Southeast Asia took note. Observations began in the early thirteenth century, primarily of the visible aspects of the political elite in the places that the Chinese visited. These included the regalia, the dais used by rulers and the ceremonial appearances of entourages when royal processions were taking place. Other visible aspects of the port cities or urban centers that the Chinese took note of included such built forms as city walls. Finally, ethnological aspects that were noted included how the locals dressed (Ptak, 1995). These were features that were visible from afar, and were noted for all the places that were recorded in Chinese texts (Figure 21).

On the other hand, aspects of social practices that may be associated with close social proximity, such as judicial systems and issues related to marriages, were only recorded for a few places in Southeast Asia. The *Zhufanzhi*, reflecting the early thirteenth century, notes information on marriage issues for only the key ports of Southeast Asia – Srivijaya-Jambi, Champa and Java (Chen & Qian, 2000: 8, 9, 46, 47, 88, 89, 101, 102). The *Daoyi zhilue*, reflecting the mid-fourteenth century, shows a minimal expansion of the places about which such information is recorded to include three additional ports in the Gulf of Siam – Khmer Cambodia (likely the Mekong River delta), Terenggani and Pahang – as well as the port of Deli in northeast Sumatra (Su, 1981: 69, 99, 102, 267). Similarly, information on judicial issues was only noted of Champa, Khmer Cambodia, Srivijaya-Jambi and Java in the *Zhufanzhi*, while information on such issues were noted in the *Daoyi zhilue* only for Khmer Cambodia. It would appear that longer-term sojourning, which would involve the possibility of marriage to local partners and dealings with the local judicial system beyond trade-related matters, was only occurring in the key entrepôts of Southeast Asia in the early thirteenth century, extending to the Gulf of Siam littoral, the Luzon area and northeast Sumatra by the mid-fourteenth century. In other words, the presence of Chinese residential agents in Southeast Asia were likely limited to these areas.

This state of affairs changed in the late fourteenth and fifteenth centuries. Following the political upheavals in China that led to the advent of Ming Dynastic rule (1368–1644), a series of maritime bans were instituted, initially

Figure 21 Angkor Thom, the religious center of the Khmer Empire during the reign of Jayavarman VII (r. 1181–1218), and contemporaneous to the *Zhufanzhi* (c.1225)

imposed on private shipping and trade, followed by an outright ban of all maritime activities from the 1440s till 1567. The knowledge accrued by the Chinese about Southeast Asia enabled merchants and shippers to relocate their activities to the region as a means of continuing their commercial activities. This led to a shift of the locus of Chinese commercial networks from south China to Southeast Asia, primarily Hoi An (central Vietnamese coast), Ayutthaya (Gulf of Siam), Palembang and Melaka (Melaka Straits) and Batavia (Java), all places about which the Chinese had already accrued some information that was critical for longer-term sojourning (Kwee, 2006 & 2013; Blussé, 2013).

Southeast Asian Networks

Underpinning all of the above commercial networks were the Southeast Asian networks themselves. The region's networks allowed for goods – forest and marine products, agricultural produce and manufactured items – to be moved from the various economic zones to the port cities, which were in turn circulated within Southeast Asia itself as well as abroad. These networks also facilitated the movement of imported items from across Maritime Asia to be redistributed to various parts of Southeast Asia.

Southeast Asia's networks consisted of three subnetworks that typically occurred within a geographical space. The first was the upstream network, which included the uplands, such as the mountainous areas, as well as the inland plains. The second was the downstream network, which included the lower reaches of a river system, such as the riparian areas and the coastlines. The third was the epicenter of the network: the port city. This epicenter would have access to the rest of the region's ports, as well as the other economic areas of Maritime Asia. Together, these three networks formed a complete economic network at the subregional level in Southeast Asia (Bronson, 1977).

Such a network could be based on a riverine system. The Musi River, for example, is fed by streams in the upland southeast slopes of the Barisan mountain range of Sumatra, with the streams coming to form the river and flowing through the lower-elevation inland areas. These areas formed the upstream economic network of the river. Natural products from these two ecological zones were gathered by the local inhabitants, and exchanged with those who would travel up from the riparian areas of the river's course. Representing the downstream network, these riparian traders would offer products obtained from their ecological zone, as well as those imported from other parts of Southeast Asia and Maritime Asia, in exchange for upstream products. Eventually, the downstream traders would trade both the products obtained from the upstream network, as well as those produced in their downstream areas, to the port city of Palembang. Palembang would then take all of these products, and make them available to foreign traders from other parts of Southeast Asia and Maritime Asia. In return, Palembang would obtain foreign products made available by these traders arriving at its port. These foreign imports would then be fed back into the upstream networks in the reverse direction (Miksic, 2009). Similar riverine economic networks may be observed along the Red River system in north Vietnam, the Batang Hari River system in Sumatra and the networks that connected the ports of the Vietnamese coast with their upland hinterlands (Watson-Andaya, 1993).

A second type of economic network, similar to the riverine system, may be observed in the maritime environment of Southeast Asia. In the case of Temasik, the port city was located on the southern tip of Singapore Island, on the north bank of the Singapore River (Heng, 1999 & 2002; Miksic, 2013). As a port, Temasik had access to products imported from south China and the Indian subcontinent, as well as the Gulf of Siam littoral (through the kingdoms of Sukhothai and Ayutthaya) and Java (through the kingdom of Majapahit) (Kwa et.al., 2019: 18–49; Heng, 2019b). Products from the seas around Singapore Island were harvested and made available to Temasik by tribes of sea people, or Orang Laut (Figure 22), who inhabited the coastal areas on

Singapore Island as well as the Riau Archipelago. These Orang Laut tribes formed the downstream segment of the larger Riau-Lingga network, of which Temasik was the epicenter (Heng, 2019a). This downstream segment connected Temasik to an upstream segment that comprised the inland areas of the Riau-Lingga islands, such as Bintan, Lingga and South Johor, as well as such South China Sea islands as Natuna and Midai off the coast of the Malay Peninsula (Miksic, 1994). The downstream Orang Laut tribes inhabiting the coasts near the port of Temasik would have obtained the products that were harvested by the inhabitants of the upstream localities, and in return would have offered products that were obtained from the areas that they inhabited, as well as foreign products that could be obtained through the port of Temasik (Heng, 1999).

Similar maritime-based economic networks may be observed along the northwest coast of the Malay Peninsula centered on South Kedah, the northeast coast of Sumatra centered on Samudra-Pasai and Lambri, and the north coast of Borneo Island and the Sulu Islands centered on Brunei (King & Druce, 2020).

A third economic network pertains to the agrarian societies of Southeast Asia. Distinct from the riverine system and maritime networks, this type of network was located in the agrarian plains of Southeast Asia. The network

Figure 22 Orang Laut family on their residential boat, known as a *tungkal* (repro-negative, c.1914) (Source: Wikimedia Commons: https://commons.wikimedia.org/wiki/File: COLLECTIE_TROPENMUSEUM_Woonschuit_ van_een_Oerang-Laoet_familie_Ka._Toengkal_TMnr_10010488.jpg)

consisted of clusters of agricultural lands that were centered around semi-urban centers such as villages and towns. Each of these centers hosted local temples, with the local economy of the lands often dedicated to the religious centers, thereby creating what may be regarded as a religious economic network. Each of these networks were spatially distributed concentrically around an epicenter, which served as the political, religious and economic hub of the agrarian landscape. The epicenter would exercise the greatest economic control over the lands that were in the immediate proximity of the epicenter, with the level of control, and therefore extraction of economic output, decreasing proportionally as the lands were located further away from the center. All the lands were in turn connected to the epicenter by networks of roads to facilitate the transportation of produce and people from the former to the latter (Tambiah, 1977; Wolters, 1999).[1] Such a network was primarily an endogenous network, although access to the external world did exist by way of a river or road that would lead to a port city located on the sea coast.

Such economic networks could be found, in the late first and early second millennia CE, in central Java, Siem Reap in present-day Cambodia, central Thailand and central Myanmar (Figure 23). The economies of these places were centered primarily on rice production, with such artisan crafts are ceramics, metalware and textiles being secondary economic activities. While some external trade did take place, these economies were primarily internally focused. The religious community, such as the Buddhist Sangha in the case of Myanmar or the temple systems of Cambodia and Java, held their respective economic systems together (Lustig, 2009; Hefner, 1990).

Intraregionally, Southeast Asia was connected economically through its seas. The various maritime subregions formed a series of commercial networks that were networked by coastal societies, which were often organized on an ethnic basis. The Malay commercial networks, which originated from the west Indonesian archipelago and the Malay Peninsula, were formed by the various Orang Laut tribes. These tribes were able to reach across to Java, the south coast of Borneo, the Gulf of Siam and the South China Sea littoral (Benjamin & Chou, 2002; Andaya, 2008: 173–201). The Bugis, on the other hand, emanated from Sulawesi. This network reached into the east Indonesian archipelago, including Sulawesi, the Spice Islands, East Java, the Sulu Zone and the Philippines (Andaya, 1995; Druce, 2009). The Dvaravati societies of the Gulf of Siam littoral maintained commercial networks that extended westward overland across the Isthmus of Kra to the Bay of Bengal littoral, inland into Mainland

---

[1] For an example of such a road system in the Angkor Kingdom, refer to https://angkordatabase .asia/links/the-living-angkor-road-project (accessed March 10, 2020). Also see Hendrickson (2010).

Figure 23 The agricultural plains of Bagan, central Myanmar, dotted with Buddhist stupas built between the ninth and thirteenth centuries, which served as the structure of the redistributive economy of Bagan (Source: Wikimedia Commons: https://commons.wikimedia.org/wiki/File:Old_Bagan,_Myanmar,_ Bagan_plains_at_sunset.jpg)

Southeast Asia and eastward into the South China Sea littoral (Mudar, 1999: 1; Vallibhotama, 1986). Finally, the Cham societies, located along the south and central Vietnamese coasts, extended their networks into the South China Sea littoral, across into the Gulf of Siam and the east coast of the Malay Peninsula, and on to the north coast of Borneo Island (Li, 2006). Taken together, these networks overlapped at their respective peripheries and linked Southeast Asia into a coherent economic sphere through its maritime waterways.

Finally, at the transregional level, state-sponsored commercial networks were responsible for connecting Southeast Asia economically to the rest of Maritime Asia. Rather than ports that received international trade due to their location as landfall sites across large maritime bodies, such as the northwest and northeast coasts of the Malay Peninsula and the Isthmus of Kra or the north coast of Sumatra, these networks enabled the states of Southeast Asia to extend their economic networks beyond the region into the key economies of Maritime Asia. As such, direct participation in international trade was limited to a small number of states with the economic means, maritime technology and navigational knowledge to sail to these foreign first-tier economies. These states also had to possess the requisite diplomatic capabilities, as the trading missions often doubled as diplomatic missions as well (Bielenstein, 2005: 1–100; Heng, 2012: 37–71).

From the mid-first millennium CE, Southeast Asian states capable of dispatching commercial missions to China included Srivijaya, Java, Champa and Cambodia. By the end of the millennium, the list of states with such capabilities expanded slightly to include North Borneo and Tambralingga. Finally, by the late twelfth century, polities that were able to reach China directly included smaller port cities on the Malay Peninsula, such as Pahang, Kuala Berang (Terengganu) and Kompei (northeast Sumatra) (Heng, 2012: 105).

Southeast Asia's network across to the Indian subcontinent was much more limited. This was likely due to the much longer distance between the subcontinent and such areas as the Vietnamese coast, the Gulf of Siam and the east Indonesian archipelago. As such, the only Southeast Asian state noted in Indian records to have crossed the Bay of Bengal was Srivijaya, even though it is likely that mariners based in the Malay Peninsula, north Sumatra, Borneo and Java sailed across the Bay of Bengal during the first millennium CE. A 1005 inscription recorded that Srivijaya had built a *vihara* (Buddhist monastery) at Nagapattinam, followed by several donations of lamps, jewelry sets and Chinese gold (presumably ornaments) between 1005 and 1019, which were carried out by agents representing the king of Srivijaya (Heng, 2012: 85; Chandra, 1957: 15; Coedes, 1918: 5). These overtures were apparently acknowledged by the Chola kings, as suggested by their memorialization in inscriptions from the relevant temples. While it does appear that Srivijaya was keen to maintain commercial relations with the states on the east coast of the Indian subcontinent, particularly the Chola port cities of Nagapattinam and Kamchipuram, the fact that only a little more than a decade after the initial donation of gold to the Indian temple to help foreign relations, the Chola navy embarked on an expedition that led to the capture of the Srivijayan ruler and his ultimate exile in India, suggests that these relations were tenuous at best (Kulke, 2009: 7–9).

By the thirteenth century, the growing dominance of Chinese shipping and merchant networks resulted in a decline in Southeast Asian states maintaining transregional networks to China. From the 1320s onwards, following the Yuan Dynasty permitting Chinese private maritime shipping and trade to take place, Southeast Asian commercial activities in the Bay of Bengal were noted to have been conducted via Chinese vessels (Heng, 2012: 64). Southeast Asian networks declined accordingly.

5 Southeast Asia's Products in Trade

The diverse nature of human societies in Southeast Asia created varying markets that would develop a diversity of demand for products not available in the local context. This included variations and differences in utilitarian needs, status signaling and size of markets as well as aesthetic tastes. Additionally, geographical factors resulted in nodal communication points being located in the maritime zone of Southeast Asia, with the inland zone dependent on the former as the means by which interactions with the external world could be effected, even as the former would depend heavily on the latter for the products that the external world would demand. The codependency between land and maritime zones has characterized the social and economic nature of Southeast Asia as a coherent whole.

However, it was not only Indigenous products that Southeast Asia exported. Given its location and role in shipping and communications in Maritime Asia, another group of trade products was also made available by Southeast Asian ports for export. These were the products obtained from other economic zones in Maritime Asia, which were transshipped to other parts of the maritime world. These included products that were unique to the cultures and areas in which they were produced. From China came ceramics, precious metal items, silk textiles, foodstuffs and specie (coinage). The Indian subcontinent was the source of cotton textiles, various types of timber, including sandalwood, earthenware ceramics as well as specie. From the Middle East and East Africa came such aromatic resins as frankincense, myrrh, liquid storax and dragon's blood, culinary liquids carried in amphorae, dates, glassware, ivory, rhinoceros horns and unique ceramic items (Schafer, 1963; Wheatley, 1961), including a type of turquoise-glazed stoneware that appeared to have been present in Southeast Asia from the ninth century onwards (Guy, 2017: 185). These products, often demanded by the markets at opposite ends of the maritime realm, would be brought to Southeast Asia's ports, where they would then be exchanged at emporiums for products from Southeast Asia as well as other places.

Finally, given that Southeast Asia served as the confluence zone of the varied Maritime Asian cultures, the region became the source of cultural and religious artifacts that were exported from their original cultural zones. Buddhist relics, Chinese gold objects, Indian astronomical instruments and mobile shrines, to name but a few such items, were often brought to and transshipped from Southeast Asia to other parts of Maritime Asia.

Although Southeast Asia had a lot to offer in terms of products available for export and reexport, the myriad shipping and merchant networks that operated in Southeast Asia did not necessarily demand or capitalize on the whole range of products. Instead, each network, representing the region from which they originated and the markets that those regions in turn served, maintained unique demand patterns of products available in Southeast Asia. Often, the demand would evolve over time, reflecting the shifting nature of commerce and market consumption patterns that the networks represented.

Middle Eastern Demand for Products in Southeast Asia

The Middle Eastern networks emanating from the west Indian Ocean, which were at their most prolific in Southeast Asia during the ninth through twelfth centuries, had begun to maintain demand for specific Southeast Asian products as early as the mid-first millennium CE. The focus, at least from the Middle Eastern textual records available on this issue, note a consistent mention of the north coast of Sumatra as an area of commercial activity in which the Middle Eastern networks were engaged. The port of Fansur, located on the northeast coast of Sumatra, appears to have had a special place in this set of textual records. The key product of interest to Middle Easterners was camphor (Donkin, 1999). This resin, obtained from the plant *Dryobalanops aromatica* (Figure 24), was different from the other type of camphor products that were sourced from elsewhere in Southeast Asia (Burkill, 1935: 862). While the camphor from Sumatra was resinous, the camphor from *Blumea balsamifera* was primarily in ground form, making the Middle Eastern demand a very specific one (Burkill, 1935: 334–339; Heng, 2015: 216–222; Wolters, 1967: 95–110).

Middle Eastern texts provide a glimpse of the kinds of Southeast Asian products that Middle Eastern traders had begun to be interested in by the end of the first millennium CE. The *Akhbar al-Sin Wa'l Hind*, for example, notes commercial interest in ambergris, used for the production of perfume and cosmetics, as well as aloeswood (Tibbetts, 1979: 26, 27). In the mid-ninth century, Ibn Khurdadhbih (850) notes that Southeast Asia produced brazilwood (a generic term for dark hardwood timber), sandalwood and bamboo. Food products that were recorded included coconuts, sugarcane, rice and bananas. For spices, cloves were mentioned. In terms of minerals, tin was noted as a product made available by Kedah (Tibbetts, 1979: 27–29).

By the tenth century, the list of products that Middle Eastern traders were interested in had grown. In terms of spices, new items mentioned included nutmeg and mace, from the eastern Indonesian archipelago, cardamom, from the Malay Peninsula, and cubeb (Figure 25), which was found in Java and Sumatra. New woods that were recorded included ebony, of which the Southeast Asian source would have been *Diospyros celebica* (Sulawesi ebony). New metals mentioned included gold from Fansur, as well as silver from Kedah (Tibbetts, 1979: 29–43).

The tenth century also witnessed an interest in fauna such as parrots, birds of paradise, peacocks and falcons, and large white monkeys were noted. Additionally, ivory was now mentioned for the first time as a product from Southeast Asia, even though Middle Eastern traders, for centuries prior to this, had access to other sources of ivory from the Indian subcontinent as well as Africa, and had been exporting them as far as China since the second half of the

Figure 24 Drawing of Borneo camphor tree (*Dryobalanops aromatica*),
flowers, leafy stem and sectioned seed. Colored zincograph, c.1853, after
M. Burnett (Source: Wellcome Collection: https://wellcomecollection.org/
works/mdh5pmtd/images?id=hz495sg3)

first millennium CE. By the twelfth century, the list of fauna products from
Southeast Asia included the musk of the civet cat (Figure 26). By the thirteenth
century, elephants were noted as well (Tibbetts, 1979: 48–60).

The sources of specific products from Southeast Asia also broadened in
tandem with the broadening of the range of products that interested Middle
Eastern traders. Initially, the few products known to them during the mid-first
millennium CE were primarily sourced from north Sumatra and the northwest
coast of the Malay Peninsula. These included the ports of Fansur and South
Kedah. By the tenth century, Cambodia had come to be known as a source of
aloeswood (Figure 27), while Srivijaya was noted to have been an important
transshipment hub of products sourced in Island Southeast Asia. By the twelfth
century, Java had become another source of products from the Indonesian
archipelago. Finally, in the fourteenth century, Cambodia became known as
the source of Mainland Southeast Asian products.

Figure 25 Drawing of cubeb, from *Köhler's Medizinal-Pflanzen in naturgetreuen Abbildungen mit kurz erläuterndem Texte: Atlas zur Pharmacopoea germanica etc.* (c.1887–1898) (Source: Wikimedia Commons: https://commons.wikimedia.org/wiki/File:Piper_cubeba_-_K%C3%B6hler% E2%80%93s_Medizinal-Pflanzen-244.jpg)

Middle Eastern interest in products available in Southeast Asia was first and foremost for the purpose of meeting the market demand back home. This notion is supported by Chinese textual information. The *Zhufanzhi* (c.1225), for example, notes that the key port of the Arabs, likely a reference to Basra, had cloves, nutmeg and putchuck (Chen & Qian, 2000: 174). At the same time, a number of products that these traders acquired were in fact intended for other markets such as China. Middle Eastern shipping and merchants heading there had to do so via Southeast Asia. The result was that products from Southeast Asia came to be included in the range of products that Middle Eastern merchants and ships brought to the Chinese ports. As early as the mid-first millennium CE, an aromatic product from the Melaka Straits region began to be demanded by Middle Eastern traders. This was benzoin, a type of resin storax obtained from

Figure 26 Ten viverrid mammals of the family *Viverridae*, including civets, from which civet musk is obtained. Colored etching by J. Miller, after Captain T. Brown (active 1842–55) (Source: Wellcome Collection: https://wellcome collection.org/works/j9jkjc73/images?id=rg73nksv)

Figure 27 *Aquilaria Malaccensis* (left), one of several species of *Aquilaria*, from which aloeswood or gharuwood (right) may be obtained; native to the Indian subcontinent, Mainland Southeast Asia and Island Southeast Asia (Source: Wikimedia Commons: https://commons.wikimedia.org/wiki/File: Aquilaria_malaccensis_-_Agar_Wood,_Eaglewood_-_Indian_ Aloewood_at_Munnar_(4).jpg and https://commons.wikimedia.org/wiki/ File:Agarwood.JPG)

the plant *styrax benzoin*, which grows primarily in Sumatra (Burkill, 1935: 758). This demand does not appear to have been generated by the Middle Eastern market. Instead, it would appear that Middle Eastern traders heading to south China had started utilizing this Southeast Asian product as a substitute for liquid storax, which was obtained from the plant *Liquidambar orientalis*, found in the east Mediterranean region. It is possible that the availability of benzoin in the Melaka Straits meant that this was a cheaper alternative to liquid storax, making the transportation of this substitute to China much easier and therefore more cost-effective than the Middle Eastern product itself.

Chinese records of state-level missions arriving at its shores provide another source of information on the Southeast Asian products obtained by Middle Eastern traders for the purpose of trade in China. In 824, a Persian mission was noted to have arrived in China, presenting a gift of gharuwood incense. The Arabs, on the other hand, likely representing the Umayyad Dynasty, presented Barus camphor in 724 (Bielenstein, 2005: 357). In 984 and 995, Arab missions presented white Barus camphor and granulated sugar (Bielenstein, 2005: 360, 361). It would appear that camphor, which was already well known to the Middle Eastern market, was another Southeast Asian product that was picked up by Middle Eastern traders and brought to China for trade.

Finally, for Middle Eastern traders, Southeast Asia was also the place where products from China could be obtained. These included ceramics and silks. A broad range of these products, which were manufactured by different kilns districts throughout south China, including the kilns of Changsha, Ding, Gongxian, Longquan, Jingdezhen and Dehua, to name but a few, could be

Figure 28 Items recovered from the Belitung wreck. (Left) Cup with drinking spout, copper-green splashes on whitesSlip, produced in the Gongxian kilns of Henan Province (Source: Wikimedia Commons: https://commons.wikimedia.org/wiki/File:Stemcup_with_duck_from_the_Belitung_shipwreck,_ArtScience_Museum,_Singapore_-_20110618.jpg)
(Right) Gold octagonal cup of Chinese manufacture, mimicking Middle Eastern design. (Source: Wikimedia Commons: https://commons.wikimedia.org/wiki/File:Octagonal_footed_gold_cup_from_the_Belitung_shipwreck,_ArtScience_Museum,_Singapore_-_20110618–02.jpg)

found at the ports of Southeast Asia, making Southeast Asia a viable source of Chinese reexport products. Chinese gold items, recovered from such wrecks as the Belitung and Nanhai 1, suggest that these items were also likely available for reexport at Southeast Asia's ports (Figure 28). Ibn Idrisi (1165) mentions, for example, that medicinal plants from China and Chinese ceramics (specifically vases) were being made available for export in Java (Tibbetts, 1979: 51–54).

South Asian Trade in Southeast Asian Products

Despite the apparent vibrancy in shipping and commercial interactions between Southeast Asia and the Indian subcontinent, there is relatively little information on the specificity of the Southeast Asian products that were demanded by South Asian traders. Gold was one of the most important products mentioned in South Asian texts in conjunction with Southeast Asia. Nonetheless, there were other Southeast Asian products that were demanded by South Asian traders through the first and early second millennia CE.

In terms of the South Asian textual corpus, one of the earliest texts, the *Silappadikaram*, a second-century CE epic poem in Tamil, mentions the arrival of ships in Madura, riding the east wind and carrying aloeswood, camphor, sandalwood and spices (Devahuti, 1965: 30). The geographical sources of the products were likely confined to one primary area – the northern end of the Melaka Straits. Camphor was sourced from north Sumatra and the Isthmus of Kra, while aloeswood, or gharuwood, was sourced from the Malay Peninsula and the Isthmus of Kra. This converges with the archaeological information on the presence of sojourning South Asian populations in Southeast Asia during the early first millennium CE, which was confined primarily to Sungei Bujang (South Kedah, Malaysia) and the east and west coasts of the Isthmus of Kra.

Indian demand for camphor continued through the first millennium CE. A seventh-century drama in Sanskrit mentions the island of camphor (Devahuti, 1965: 31). While sandalwood (*Santalum album*) is found on the Indian subcontinent, Southeast Asia, especially the east Indonesian archipelago, has historically been known as a source of this aromatic wood. While the *Silappadikaram* does not go into detail as to which spices were being referred to in the poem, it is possible that the products were the ones Island Southeast Asia was known for during this time, such as cloves (Figure 29) and nutmeg. These would have also been products sourced from the east Indonesian archipelago.

By the early second millennium CE, additional products from Island Southeast Asia, particularly the east Indonesian archipelago, were noted to have been demanded by South Asian traders. The Tanjore inscription, dated to 1030 and commemorating the naval expedition sent by Rajendra Chola I to the Melaka Straits region around 1025, mentions sandalwood incense as a product made available by the port cities located there (Subbarayalu, 2009: 160). Additionally, Chinese texts record that in 1077, a Chola mission presented camphor and cloves to the Song court (Bielenstein, 2005: 78). Finally, a Tamil inscription, found in Barus (north Sumatra) and dated to 1088, records that the payment of docking charges for South Asian vessels at that port was to be paid in gold, based on the prevailing price of musk (Christie, 1998: 258). This suggests that musk was a local product that was acquired by Indian traders by this time.

By the fourteenth century, a few more products were added to the repertoire of items sourced from Southeast Asia. The Kovilpatti inscription, dated to 1305, mentions sandalwood paste, camphor, areca nuts, rhinoceros horns, musk, tamarind and cinnamon (Karashima, 2009: 141). While sandalwood paste, areca nuts and cinnamon could have been sourced from South Asia as well, the remaining products on the list were likely obtained primarily from Southeast Asia. Additionally, two fourteenth-century commentaries on the epic poem *Silappadikaram* identify the spices carried by the vessels riding the east wind to Madura as cloves and cubeb. This likely reflected the trade maintained by Indian traders during the mid-second millennium CE (Devahuti, 1965: 30, 31).

Figure 29 Drawing of a clove tree, from *Tractado de las drogas, y medicinas de las Indias Orientales, con sus plantas debuxadas al biuo por Christoual Acosta ... En el qual se verifica mucho de lo que escriuio el doctor Garcia de Orta* by Cristóbal Acosta and Garcia de Orta (c.1578) (Source: Wellcome Collection: https://wellcomecollection.org/works/wwhk5sdt/images? id=zppjbq9 v)

Chinese Trade in Southeast Asian Products

Of the cultural regions that were in contact and interaction with Southeast Asia in premodernity, China was the most important foreign trading partner. The geographical proximity between the two regions resulted, as early as the beginning of the first millennium CE, in the development of a more broad-based and intimate knowledge of the products that each region could make available to the other than any of the other regions that were in contact with Southeast Asia up to the early modern era. The continuity of the landmass from south China through to Mainland Southeast Asia meant that there was a continuity in the transition between the ecological zones from the former, which were located well in the subtropical belt, to the latter, of which the southern regions were located in the equatorial tropical zone.

The result was that the Chinese and Southeast Asians shared many common types of natural resources. These included flora and fauna products, as well as minerals. As an example, the Sanxingdui hoard in Sichuan Province, which is a late Shang period Bronze Age site dated to the end of the second millennium BCE, contained a large cache of elephant tusks (Figure 30) along with bronze items and jade articles (Ge & Linduff, 1990). The tusks were likely obtained from elephants that would have roamed the subtropical areas of south China during that time, and were therefore likely to have been a local item. But by the first millennium CE, China's supply of ivory was entirely sourced from abroad, including Southeast Asia, the Indian subcontinent and Africa (Elvin, 2008). The commonalty of the ancient geographical distribution of ivory both in China and Southeast Asia meant that ivory's uses, including as a prized material for decorative arts and ritual purposes, caused its adoption and usage to be seamless over a long period of time.

Another, more recent example would be lakawood (Figure 31) (Heng, 2001). By the late tenth century, this aromatic wood had become noted by the Song

Figure 30 Ivory tusk, excavated from Sanxingdui, Sichuan Province, China, dated to the late second millennium CE (late Shang period) (Source: Wikimedia Commons: https://commons.wikimedia.org/wiki/File:Sanxingdui_Ivory_Tusk_ (9951099014).jpg)

court as one among a range of Southeast Asian products imported by China through the South China Sea route. Lakawood grew in importance, such that by the early thirteenth century, the Maritime Shipping Superintendent at Quanzhou – Zhao Rugua – noted in the *Zhufanzhi* that this aromatic wood, which was very cheap to obtain, had become such a widely used ingredient for the manufacture of joss sticks that even poor people were able to afford it. The same text notes, however, that the lakawood plant used to grow widely throughout Guangdong and Guangxi but that, due to deforestation and overharvesting, it had become extinct in south China by the end of the first millennium CE (Chen & Qian, 2000: 368). Indeed, the *Nanfang caomuzhuang*, a pharmabotanical treatise published in the fourth century CE, describes the lakawood plant as a native of subtropical south China (Li, 1979: 103). Again, it would appear that Chinese familiarity with the product, derived from a plant whose geographical distribution covered both south China and Southeast Asia, enabled the Southeast Asian version to be readily imported and adopted by the Chinese once the product became known and was made available to them.

During the mid-first millennium CE, several key Southeast Asian products were imported by China, for which Chinese textual documents provide consistent mention. In terms of flora products, China was importing camphor, benzoin, sappanwood, gharuwood, cloves, nutmeg and betel nuts (Bielenstein, 2005: 82–98). With the exception of gharuwood, these were products that were used in Chinese medicinal treatments. Gharuwood, which was a generic term used for a broad range of aromatic woods of the genus *Aquilaria* that attained their

Figure 31 Picture of lakawood pieces, obtained from *Dalbergia parviflora*, shown with a box of matches, indicating the wood is to be lit as incense. Image from the Nationaal Museum van Wereldculturen, Netherlands (Source: Wikimedia Commons: https://commons.wikimedia.org/wiki/File:COLLECTIE_TROPENMUSEUM_ Stukken_Laka_hout_(reukhout)_naast_luciferdoosje_TMnr_10006244.jpg)

fragrant qualities through the process of humification, was likely used as incense, as well as material for the fashioning of decorative items, including furniture. Sappanwood (*Biancaea sappan*) was imported as a dyestuff and likely used as a red colorant. Of these products, benzoin and camphor were sourced from Sumatra, even though camphor was also produced in Mainland Southeast Asia. Cloves and nutmeg would have been available only from the east Indonesian archipelago. All the other products, while also available from Island Southeast Asia, were products of Mainland Southeast Asia as well.

The two main Southeast Asian animal products that the Chinese were familiar with and imported during this time were ivory and rhinoceros horn. The former had already been known to the Chinese as an expensive artisan craft material, while the latter had begun to be used as an ingredient in Chinese medicinal treatments. The importation of both items has primarily been recorded in the context of state-level missions that were received by the Tang court. The other Southeast Asian products identified in Tang period texts as items that had been brought by state-level missions were gold ornaments and jewelry, and pearls. These were presented primarily by missions from Linyi (present-day south Vietnam) (Bielenstein, 2005: 36–40). In this regard, the source of precious fauna materials from Southeast Asia was Linyi, suggesting that this was an extension of Chinese demand for products that they were already familiar with within their geographical setting.

With the advent of the Song Dynasty, China's import of Southeast Asian products grew substantially. In a 976 memorial, several new Southeast Asian products were noted to have been imported. These included pearls, coral, turtle carapaces, tortoise shells and ebony. Within a decade, that list had grown to include lac, two new varieties of gharuwood (huangshou and chen) and cardamom. By the eleventh century, state-level missions from Southeast Asia were also bringing pepper and two other varieties of gharuwood (jian and su) (Heng, 2012: 140). By the end of the eleventh century, the *Pingzhou ketan* notes that sandalwood incense was imported from the Melaka Straits region port of Srivijaya to China (Heng, 2006: 12). The above developments suggest that, over the course of the late tenth and eleventh centuries, the scope of China's import of Southeast Asian products expanded geographically from just coastal south Vietnam to Island Southeast Asia, particularly the Melaka Straits region and Java.

Up until the late eleventh century, Chinese prohibition of private shipping operating beyond its coastal areas meant that the Southeast Asian products that China imported were primarily brought by foreign traders and ships. Because the interaction that foreign traders had with the Chinese was confined to the port cities of south China, and often limited to the port areas and foreign quarters of these cities, foreign knowledge of the consumption tastes of the Chinese was limited to the few products that were already tried and tested. In 1090, however, Chinese shipping was finally permitted to sail abroad from any location along the South Chinese coast for up to nine months to engage in trade. This liberalization, coupled with the reduction of the compulsory purchase and customs rates of imported products to their lowest levels in history, led to an expansion in Chinese trading activities in Southeast Asia. The result was that the range of Southeast Asian products that the Chinese imported grew exponentially through the course of the twelfth century (Heng, 2012: 48–51). A 1133 memorial on China's maritime trade noted that musk wood (i.e. musk-scented wood), rattan, timber coated with camphor paste, coconut-fiber mats and beeswax were being imported (Heng, 2012: 196, 197). The first three products were furniture construction materials, while the last was used for the manufacture of candles. Textile products, including woven mats and blankets, were also noted on the list. These were partially processed products. They were also not high-cost items. Eight years later, in 1141, a memorial recording the Song court's maritime trade policies and commercial rules listed around three hundred and sixty products that were involved in the China trade. Products imported from Southeast Asia included civet musk, damar products (resinous products derived from the plants of the *dipterocarpaceae* and *burseraceae* genus, found in the Malay Peninsula and Indonesian archipelago), two new varieties of gharuwood (sheng and zhan), nine different varieties of camphor products and three different types of rattan, as well as cotton textile items (Heng 2012: 197).

The 1090 liberalization of Chinese shipping enabled Chinese traders and mariners to gain a greater familiarity with Island Southeast Asia. Through the twelfth century, Chinese ships appear to have only headed to the key entrepôts of Southeast Asia, such as Srivijaya (southeast Sumatra), Champa (coastal South-central Vietnam) and Tambralingga (west coast of the Isthmus of Kra) This state of affairs is reflected in the list of Southeast Asian states that were recorded in the *Lingwai daida* in the late twelfth century, which contains information on the maritime activities and knowledge of the Chinese in south China (Tu, 1996: 37, 38, 42). By the early thirteenth century, however, they had begun to operate in the north Melaka Straits region, as well as the north Javanese coast. The *Zhufanzhi*, for example, notes the availability of tin and pearls from Kompei, a port located on the northeast tip of Sumatra (Chen & Qian, 2000: 78). The tin was likely sourced from the inland reaches of Sumatra as well as across the Melaka Straits from South Kedah, while the pearls would have been obtained from the nearby littoral areas of the eastern Bay of Bengal. Additionally, the Chinese had begun to assign specific qualities to the products that were available at the various Southeast Asian ports. Chinese traders were no longer just broadening the range of products they could import from Southeast Asia but also differentiating products by their respective quality, and therefore value, as well (Heng, 2008: 46–48).

By the beginning of the fourteenth century, China's demand for Southeast Asian products was very well established. The *Dade nanhaizhi*, a local geographical gazetteer published in 1306 on the Nanhai district, of which the port city of Guangzhou was a part, noted sixty-nine products that were imported through the port by that time. Of these, forty were products from Southeast Asia (Heng, 2012: 206). None of these products were recent additions, with two exceptions – hornbill casques and red-purple timber. The former was the keratin horn of the helmeted hornbill (Figure 32) (*Rhinoplax vigil*), whose geographical distribution spanned Sumatra, the Malay Peninsula and Borneo (Burkill, 1935: 1194, 1195). The latter was likely a generic term used to refer to construction timber with a red-purple hue (Heng, 2001: 142–147).

One of the most important sources of information on the Chinese trade in Southeast Asian products is from the Quanzhou wreck, dated to the 1270s. The wreck, which had called at Houtu Harbor in Quanzhou Bay (present-day Fujian Province), was carrying a cargo of Southeast Asian products when it foundered. The cargo comprised sandalwood, gharuwood, lakawood, pepper (Figure 33) and betel nuts (Merwin, 1977: 18–25). These were products from the Melaka Straits region and Java. It would appear that by the end of the thirteenth century,

Figure 32 The helmeted hornbill (*Rhinoplax vigil*) (Source: Wikimedia Commons: https://commons.wikimedia.org/wiki/File:Rhinoplax_vigil.jpg).

these two regions of Island Southeast Asia had become the most important sources from which the Chinese obtained products. This pattern of trade would continue well into the fifteenth century.

6 Southeast Asia's Economic Integration with Maritime Asia

Given the intensity of interaction between Southeast Asia and the different regions of Maritime Asia, a certain degree of integration in the economies was bound to occur. A number of factors affected the nature and degree of Southeast Asia's economic integration with the Middle East, the Indian subcontinent and China. These included the similarities and complementarity of the natural resources, the differences in production technology and techniques, and the consumption patterns of the regions' markets.

In the first instance, geographical proximity between two regions would, at least on the surface, provide a context for some degree of economic integration. The closer two regions are located geographically, the likelier their economies would be to converge due to the intensity of interaction that comes from a relatively shorter distance between them. For instance, the east coast of the Indian subcontinent and south China are located closest to Southeast Asia. A return voyage would have been achieved, from Southeast Asia, within one monsoon cycle, or approximately six to nine months. By contrast, a return voyage from Southeast Asia to the Middle East would have taken two monsoon cycles, or around one-and-a-half years. That difference in voyage time would have meant that Southeast Asia's economy would have been more in sync with that of south China and the eastern seaboard of the Indian subcontinent than the Persian Gulf or the Red Sea (Abu-Lughod, 1989: 33–36).

A second factor, that of the geographical resources available in the respective regions, also plays a part in determining the degree of integration of two economic regions. The ecological context, and therefore the flora and fauna resources at the disposal of human societies located in the respective regions, could share similarities that would have pitted two closely located regions in direct competition with each other. As an example, the Indian subcontinent and Southeast Asia shared many common or similar products. These included such flora products that were in high demand and circulation in Maritime Asia as sandalwood, pepper, cinnamon, gharuwood and cassia bark, and such fauna products as ivory. The geographical distribution of these products extended from the Indian subcontinent through to Southeast Asia. Rather than economic integration, the commercial networks from both regions would have competed intensely for market share in exporting these products to other Maritime Asian economies such as China. The 1025 Chola naval invasion of the Melaka Straits, which targeted the port cities of the region, has been framed by scholars as an attempt by the Chola Kingdom to destabilize the commercial capabilities of the Southeast Asian ports, which would in turn have accorded an advantage to the Chola commercial networks that were operating across the Bay of Bengal and through to south China. It is worth noting that one of the most important trades that the port state of Srivijaya (southeast Sumatra) was engaged in was that of sandalwood, with China as the main recipient market. The Indian commercial networks would have been competing for this slice of the commercial pie as well. The same competitive dynamic would be witnessed later on, when Sumatra and the Indian subcontinent would compete in the production and trade in pepper in the late fourteenth century (Bulbeck et al., 1998).

Geographical proximity would be a positive factor if complementarity came with a close convergence of natural resources from two regions located close to each

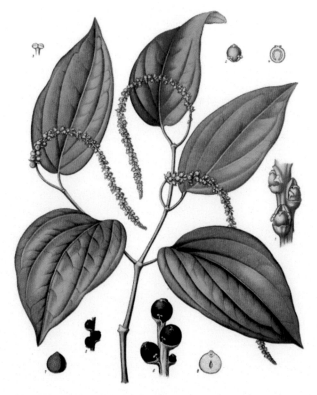

Figure 33 Natural history drawing of black pepper, from *Köhler's Medizinal-Pflanzen in naturgetreuen Abbildungen mit kurz erläuterndem Texte: Atlas zur Pharmacopoea germanica etc.* (c.1887–98) (Source: Wikimedia Commons: https://commons.wikimedia.org/wiki/File:Piper_nigrum_-_K%C3%B6hler% E2%80%93s_Medizinal-Pflanzen-107.jpg)

other. In this regard, a product available from one region, whose characteristics were sufficiently similar to a product from the other region, would be adopted for local use by the latter region's people. In this situation, product substitution would foster economic integration, as a resource found both locally and in the neighboring region would be used interchangeably. One example of such product substitution was the hornbill casque, found in Borneo, the Malay Peninsula and Sumatra. The hornbill casque had similar physical properties to ivory. Ivory was known in south China as early as the second millennium BCE, where the local geographical distribution of elephants in that area at that time resulted in the use of ivory for the production of decorative items that carried social significance. Consequently, ivory had come to be highly prized in Chinese artisan craft, with the material being imported from Southeast Asia as well as the Indian subcontinent and the Middle East through the first and second millennia CE. In the fourteenth century, the hornbill casque appeared as a trade item that was exported to China. This material was used in the production of small carved decorative items (Figure 34), similar to small ivory carvings, with the added quality of the reddish keratin that was inherent in the hornbill casque but not in ivory, and gave the former material an aesthetic edge over the former (Beavitt, 1992; Cammanns, 1951; Kwa et al., 2019: 44).

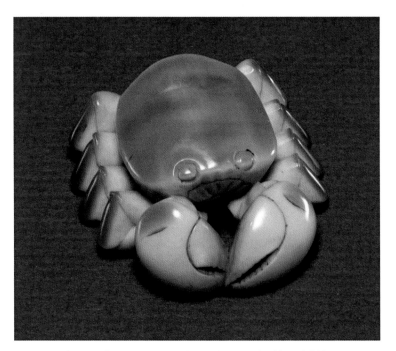

Figure 34 Nineteenth-century netsuke crab carved of hornbill ivory (Source: Wikimedia Commons: https://commons.wikimedia.org/wiki/File:Jugyoku_-_ Crab_-_Walters_71851_-_Top.jpg)

Another example of such product substitution was lakawood. Lakawood, or *Dalbergia parviflora*, is a Southeast Asian liana that has been used in Southeast Asia primarily as an incense wood due to its aromatic quality and widespread availability. Chinese texts of the first and early second millennia CE, however, note that a plant with similar qualities had, at one time, proliferated in south China. The plant, and its use as an incense wood, was a South Chinese practice well before Southeast Asian lakawood was exported to China. Southeast Asian lakawood became a major trade product only in the Song period, with the growth in its export to China occurring from the thirteenth century onwards. By the fifteenth century, the product had become such an important export item to China that it was presented to the Ming court as tribute through the imperial fleet of Admiral Zheng He (Heng, 2001: 146). Its qualities were so similar to the native South Chinese plant that it was adopted for the same uses. Lakawood's cheap price also meant that it was used by all economic strata of Chinese society (Hirth & Rockhill, 1970: 211).

Product substitution may also be seen in the reverse. An example would be camphor. The primary reason for the use of camphor by the Chinese was the unique characteristics of the terpenoid organic chemical compound. Camphor was known in Chinese texts as early as the first millennium BCE. However, the material was confined primarily to timber for carpentry and construction, and was obtained from the camphor tree of the *Lauracceae* family, which may be found in the subtropical coastal zone and outlying islands of south China (Donkin, 1999: 61–64)). Camphor as a resin was first introduced into China when it was presented to the Sui court (589–618) as a tribute item by a foreign state (Heng, 2015: 217). This was obtained from the plant *Dryobalanops aromatica* – Bornean camphor (Burkill, 1935: 862). Chinese acceptance and demand for Southeast Asian camphor appears to have come as a result of the camphor timber usage that the Chinese had originally developed. Its use was then extended to medical applications (Heng, 2015: 216–222).

In the late eleventh century, a new form of camphor began to be exported to China. Chinese records note that camphor oil was submitted by such Southeast Asian states as Srivijaya in the 1070s and 1080s as a tribute item to the Song court (Heng, 2012: 195). This oil continued to be featured as a product that was sourced from Southeast Asia through the twelfth and thirteenth centuries. This product was likely a distillate of *Blumea balsamifera* (Figure 35), which may be found in China south of the Yangzi River, although it is prevalent throughout Southeast Asia. Its use in China during the twelfth and thirteenth centuries continued to be primarily medicinal in nature. However, the acceptance and use of camphor oil from Southeast Asia appear to have precipitated China's own development of camphor oil from plant sources found within its boundaries. By the fourteenth

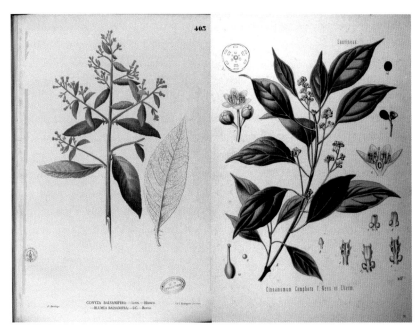

Figure 35 (Left) Illustration of the *Blumea balsamifera*, from *Flora de Filipinas* by Manuel Blanco, Celestino Fernández-Villar and Andrés Naves, c.1877 (Source: Wikimedia Commons: https://commons.wikimedia.org/wiki/File: Blumea_balsamifera_Blanco2.403-original.png) (Right) Illustration of the *Cinnamomum camphora* (from *Köhler's Medizinal-Pflanzen in naturgetreuen Abbildungen mit kurz erläuterndem Texte: Atlas zur Pharmacopoea germanica etc.*, c.1887–98) (Source: Wikimedia Commons: https://commons.wikimedia.org/wiki/File:K%C3%B6hler%27s_Medizinal-Pflanzen_in_naturgetreuen_Abbildungen_mit_kurz_erl%C3%A4uterndem_Texte_(Plate_76)_(6972254584).jpg)

century, the import trade in Southeast Asian camphor had declined, and by the fifteenth century, the trade had disappeared. In its place, the Chinese had begun to produce a distillate from the plant *Cinnamomum camphora* (Figure 35), which is found in subtropical China and Taiwan Island (Heng, 2015: 222).

The use of camphor never diminished in China. China continued into the nineteenth century to be one of the most important producers of camphor in the world. Instead, what was initially a quality or characteristic of a type of locally sourced timber used in China in the first millennium BCE became the basis of familiarity upon which a new product from Southeast Asia could be introduced. The new product was then incorporated into medicinal practice, which was completely different from the product's original use. This new usage then led to the introduction of a processed variety, which ultimately led to the development of a domestic substitute by the Chinese themselves. Economic integration was likely to have been so intense that knowledge of the production process of a product would have been transferred from one region to the other.

Economic integration could also occur as a result of the differing manufacturing capabilities of the respective regions. Here, differences in manufacturing technologies and manufacturing techniques could lead to market demand in one region for products that either were not produced locally, or were significantly different from those produced locally. As an example, vitrified stoneware (ceramics fired to at least 1250 degrees Celsius), which was produced in China as early as the first millennium BCE, was a product that was unique to China in the context of large-scale ceramic production in Maritime Asia in the first and early second millennia CE. While Southeast Asian kilns had produced high-fired stoneware as early as the ninth century, most of these kilns were located inland, with relatively limited access to the international trading networks that crisscrossed Southeast Asia.

Consequently, through the first and early second millennia CE, China remained the only viable source of vitrified stoneware ceramics for Southeast Asia, and indeed the rest of Maritime Asia. As such, Southeast Asia's ceramic consumption patterns can be tied very closely to the production capabilities of south China's kiln districts. The consumption patterns reflected the evolution of ceramic production methods, including the types of glazes, clays and forms (Figure 36). The different societies of Southeast Asia also developed preferences for specific sources and forms of Chinese ceramics. In turn, China's kilns geared their ceramic production to meet this important source of market demand, producing items and forms, as well as decorations, that would appeal to Southeast Asian tastes (Ho, 2001).

The integration of the ceramics industry of south China and the demand for these ceramics in Southeast Asia may be seen in the shipwrecks of the late first and early second millennia CE from both regions that were carrying cargo from China to Southeast Asia when they foundered. The Cirebon wreck (late ninth century), for example, was carrying around 150,000 pieces of Chinese ceramics as part of its cargo, the majority of which were Yue ware (Liebner, 2014: 113). The Pulau Buaya wreck (twelfth century) was carrying around 32,000 pieces of ceramics, the bulk of which were Qingbai ware (Ridho & McKinnon, 1998: 6). The Nanhai 1 wreck (thirteenth century), a Chinese vessel on its way from south China to Southeast Asia when it foundered, was carrying approximately 80,000 pieces of ceramics, the majority of which were celadon and white ware from Fujian and Zhejiang, when it sank off the Pearl River Delta near Guangzhou (Guojia wenwuju, 2017). The Java Sea wreck (thirteenth century), a Southeast Asian vessel that was en route to Java when it sank off Belitung Island in the west Java Sea, was

Figure 36 Chinese ceramics exported to Southeast Asia. (Clockwise, from top left) Changsha bowls (Hunan Province), ninth century CE (Source: Wikimedia Commons: https://commons.wikimedia.org/wiki/File:Changsha_bowls_ from_the_Belitung_shipwreck,_ArtScience_Museum,_Singapore_-_20110319– 03.jpg); Yue bowl (Zhejiang Province), tenth century CE (Source: Wikimedia Commons: https://commons.wikimedia.org/wiki/File:Five_Dynasties_ to_Northern_Song_Yue-Ware_Celadon_Bowl_(10180406444).jpg); Qingbai dish (Jiangxi Province), twelfth century CE (Source: Wikimedia Commons: https:// commons.wikimedia.org/wiki/File:China,_Southern_Song_Dynasty_(1127– 1279)_-_Yuan_Dynasty_-_Saucer-_Qingbai_ware_-_1917.257_-_Cleveland_ Museum_of_Art.tif); Longquan foliated platter (Zhejiang Province), thirteenth– fourteenth century CE (Source: Wikimedia Commons: https://commons.wikimedia .org/wiki/File:Foliated_Dish_with_Peonies_and_Vertical_Ribs_LACMA_M .84.213.350.jpg)

carrying approximately 200,000 pieces of Chinese ceramics, the majority of which were celadon, green and white ware, as part of its cargo (Heng, 2018: 16). Finally, the Temasik wreck (fourteenth century), likely a Chinese vessel, was carrying a substantial cargo of Longquan celadon ware and Jingdezhen blue and white porcelain when it sank of the island of Pedra Branca near Singapore (Flecker, 2022). Even vessels plying intraregional routes in Southeast Asia were carrying substantial amounts of Chinese ceramics. The Intan wreck, a Southeast Asian vessel dated to the early tenth century, was en route from Sumatra to Java, and carrying around three tons of Chinese ceramics, when it foundered in the west Java Sea (Flecker, 2002: 246).

Southeast Asian societies did possess the capabilities to produce ceramics. High-fired earthenware was produced by the kilns of Mainland Southeast Asia from at least the late ninth century. Indeed, the Pulau Buaya wreck cargo comprised a number of fine-paste high-fired earthenware *kendi*s (Figure 37) (Ridho & McKinnon, 1998: 64–67; Rooney, 2003).

In Island Southeast Asia, there were societies capable of producing large numbers of earthenware vessels. At the habitation site of Temasik, a late thirteenth- to early fifteenth-century port polity located at the Singapore River on Singapore Island, earthenware vessel sherds (Figure 38) account for 10 to 20 percent of the total ceramic sherds recovered archaeologically from this settlement, even as high-fired Chinese ceramics account for around 12 to 14 percent of the total ceramic sherds recovered from this settlement (Heng, 2012: Tables B1 & B2; Chen, 2004; Lim, 2012: Table 1).

Figure 37 Earthenware *kendi*, a type of waterpot produced in Southeast Asia; this example is from Majapahit, Java, dated to the fourteenth century CE (Source: Wikimedia Commons: https://commons.wikimedia.org/wiki/File: 14th_century_Kendi_pot_(Indonesia).jpg)

Figure 38 Earthenware sherds excavated from the National Gallery site, Temasik period, Singapore (Source: Author)

In effect, Chinese high-fired ceramics did not replace Southeast Asian ceramics, even though the low unit value of the former could have easily led to such an outcome. Instead, the uses of Chinese ceramics complemented locally produced counterparts, allowing for a richer material culture and cultural articulation and practice to occur. Uses for such ceramics would include culinary, ceremonial and ritual practices, economic circulation, as well as for the expression of ethnic and social hierarchical differences (Heng, 2019b: 478–481). Mass-scale production of Southeast Asian high-fired ceramics, and with the iron-oxide glazes that often accompanied their Chinese counterparts, did not take place in Southeast Asia until the late fourteenth century, when the kilns of Sukhothai and Sawankalok in Thailand, followed by Vietnam (Figure 39), began producing such ceramics in large numbers (Hein, 2001) and exported them to the rest of Southeast Asia because of the maritime ban on Chinese shipping and trade imposed by the Ming court in China from 1371 onwards.

Differences or uniqueness in manufacturing techniques also led to economic integration between two regions. As an example, cotton cloth was produced in both Southeast Asia and the Indian subcontinent through the late first and early second millennia CE. However, the print quality of Indian cotton textiles, as well as the quality of the fabric itself, set Indian cotton textiles apart from the ones produced in Southeast Asia. Consequently, even though Indian textiles were more expensive than locally produced textiles in Southeast Asia, they were in high demand. Apart from the higher value due to the cost of importing such textiles, the quality and exclusivity of Indian textiles conferred prestige on the articles as well. In this regard, Southeast Asian societies' use of textiles, for ceremonial and ritual purposes and for the articulation of social status, as well as the similarities in the textiles produced, enabled Indian textiles to be adopted and incorporated into local usage patterns, and perhaps enhanced the articulation of social practices (Hall, 1996).

Figure 39 Southeast Asian high-fired ceramics exported to the rest of Southeast Asia from the late fourteenth century CE onward. (Clockwise from top left) Si Satchanalai celadon bowl (Thailand) (Source: Wikimedia Commons: https:// commons.wikimedia.org/wiki/File:Bowl_with_Incised_Peony_Designs_ LACMA_AC1997.252.1.jpg); Sawankhalok Celadon Platter (Thailand), fifteenth century CE (Source: Wikimedia Commons: https://commons.wikimedia.org/ wiki/File:Bowl_LACMA_M.84.213.34.jpg); Annamese blue and white platter (Vietnam), fifteenth–sixteenth century CE (Source: The Metropolitan Museum of Art: https://www.metmuseum.org/art/collection/search/40001); Si Satchanalai lidded pot with underglaze decoration (Thailand), fourteenth–sixteenth century CE (Source: Wikimedia Commons: https://commons.wikimedia.org/wiki/File: British_Museum_Asia_2_(cropped).jpg)

Finally, economic integration could occur when the scale of manufacturing employed in the producing region allowed for sheer cost savings in the recipient region, even though the latter might possess the requisite technology to produce similar items. Chinese iron products serve as a useful example here. Even though Southeast Asian societies in Mainland Southeast Asia and certain parts of Island Southeast Asia, such as the Malay Peninsula, possessed iron-smelting abilities by the early first millennium CE, during the late first and early second millennia CE, China came to be an important source of cast iron for Southeast Asia. The economies of scale enjoyed by China's iron-manufacturing industry enabled the unit cost of imported iron from China to be much more affordable than locally produced iron products from Southeast Asia. Finished products included woks and cauldrons. Partially worked iron products included trapezoidal iron bars, likely used for producing swords at such iron-deficient places such as Java (Hall, 2011b), and iron rods, which may have been imported by Southeast Asian societies as raw material for metal-working activities. Consequently, the cargoes of shipwrecks comprised large quantities of Chinese iron products. The Cirebon wreck, for example, contained several stacks of iron bars in its cargo hold (Liebner, 2014: 203, 204). The Pulau Buaya wreck was carrying a cargo of several tons of iron trapezoidal bars, as well as several tons of iron woks (Ridho & McKinnon, 1998: 84). Finally, the Java Sea wreck was carrying approximately two hundred tons of iron products as part of its cargo (Mathers & Flecker, 1997: 77–79). In this regard, the low unit cost of iron, and the consequent large-scale importation of this product substitute, led not only to the influence of culinary practices in Southeast Asia through the widespread adoption of Chinese cooking vessels but also to the development of supply chains in the production of such iron items of local use (Heng, 2013: 498, 499).

The abovementioned are just several examples of the economic integration that occurred during the late first and early second millennia CE between Southeast Asia and its economic partners. Economic integration did not simply involve the import and use of a foreign product. Instead, the adoption of a product affected the recipient society by affecting the nature of material consumption culture. Often, it led to the development of new ways of doing things. It also contributed to the development of cultural nuances and vocabulary, in both language and physical articulation, in the discourse and expression of aesthetics, social status and ritual. Additionally, the reliance on the import of specific products used as materials in value-added manufacturing activities made the source of the materials an integral part of the manufacturing supply chain. It is conceivable that any disruption in the supply of materials in one region would in turn have disrupted the output of the final product, not to mention the economic repercussions on the industry and economic sector, of the other region.

7 Conclusion

What we have called, for convenience, the Global Middle Ages was a period of increasing wealth, due to the increase in agricultural output and workforce resulting from the Medieval Warm Period. Coupled with the relatively diffused geopolitical contexts of the Asian continent, this led to an uptick in exchanges and interactions across Asia during the mid-first to early second millennium CE. The growth in interactions was facilitated, at least in Maritime Asia, by the preexisting navigational technology and knowledge that the societies possessed. Transregional exchanges were made possible by the continental monsoon wind patterns, which facilitated the movement of large numbers of people and goods, and led to the dissemination of cultures across this maritime space.

Southeast Asia played a key role in this global exchange. First, it served as an economic and cultural zone in its own right on the Maritime Asian exchange map. Second, it served as a conduit, facilitating the interactions between other zones in Maritime Asia. This was made possible by the legacy of maritime navigation in Southeast Asia, which had developed since prehistoric times. Economic exchanges in premodernity rode on the legacy of the region's history of commerce, which, at least in the Bay of Bengal littoral and coastal south China, was evident from the first millennium BCE. This continuous history of commerce and trade, which engaged all of Southeast Asia, including the Indonesian archipelago, was facilitated by the trade winds or easterlies, which allowed for maritime navigation across all of Maritime Southeast Asia, thereby enabling the involvement of even the eastern extremities of the region in the global exchange by the mid-first millennium CE.

For Southeast Asia, the uniqueness of this premodern period as an international context allowed for a diversity of networks to operate in and across the region. Through the course of the mid-first to early second millennium CE, different shipping networks operated in Southeast Asia. These networks facilitated the commercial needs of the respective regions from which they originated. At times, they also facilitated the needs of the regions in which they were operating. As such, Middle Eastern shipping facilitated the commercial needs of Southeast Asia and China, both of which were regions in which these vessels were located. Indian shipping facilitated the exchange needs of Southeast Asia, and to a lesser extent China as well. By the thirteenth century, Chinese shipping had begun to do the same in Southeast Asia and across the Bay of Bengal.

The shipping networks were supplemented by organized commercial networks, such as guilds, which established sojourning communities and commercial agencies at the port cities of Southeast Asia. These communities brought with them, and perpetuated in these port cities, the cultural practices of their respective home regions. Investment in the port cities in which commercial agents resided, including the construction of religious buildings such as temples and infrastructural projects such as ritual tanks, as well as the establishment of intangible cultural traits such as languages and commercial practices, including taxation and customs duties rules, occurred in Southeast Asia.

The extent to which the different commercial networks invested in the port cities of Southeast Asia varied significantly. Those that were highly organized and institutionalized, particularly with state involvement, such as the Indian networks, tended to sink deeper roots into the places where they established sojourning communities. Other networks that relied primarily on private capital, such as the Chinese networks, do not appear to have seen the need for a similar degree of commitment to the Southeast Asian ports. Presumably, the relatively close proximity of the two regions, China and Southeast Asia, coupled with the need for immediate profit maximization due to the predominance of diffused private capital driving the commercial exchanges, appears to have led to a minimum of long-term investments in the port cities of Southeast Asia by the Chinese trading communities. The typical length of time of sojourns in Southeast Asia by the people belonging to the various networks that operated there was likely to have been different.

Over the long period of what we have called the Global Middle Ages, Southeast Asia grew in importance as a source of products demanded by the world. The range of products made available went from a few high-value products in the mid-first millennium CE to a broad range of products of varying values by the twelfth century. Southeast Asia's products were not only sought after by traders from their respective home markets; they were also acquired as part of the transshipment trade to other markets that demanded them. The products traded ranged from ready-to-use items to raw materials needed as manufacturing ingredients or for artisan crafts.

The interconnectedness across Maritime Asia and Southeast Asia allowed for different types of economic integration to occur over time. Southeast Asia experienced, with its various trading partner regions, vertical economic integration in which the primary, secondary and even service industries of another region were integrated with Southeast Asia's. Economic codependencies also developed, with specific regions often serving as the primary source of specific products, such as high-fired ceramics, furniture-making materials, textiles and metal items. Even shared common currency spheres occurred. Indian currencies were utilized across both sides of the Bay of Bengal, while Chinese copper cash was in circulation and used in market transactions both in China and in large areas of Southeast Asia, including Java, Sumatra and Cambodia.

Overall, the Global Middle Ages was a period of integration and interaction for the economies of Southeast Asia and Maritime Asia. There was consistent growth in the global economy, particularly from the ninth through the thirteenth centuries. By the time the European networks, represented by the Portuguese and the Spaniards, appeared on the scene in Southeast Asia in the early sixteenth century, they were witnessing an integrated transregional economy that was connected at the continental level. This provided the context in which European colonialism, and the global colonial economies of European imperialism, could then be established in the modern era. As it was during premodernity, Southeast Asia continued to play the role of a nexus region, and a key player, in the global modern era.

References

Abraham, M. (1988). *Two Medieval Merchant Guilds of South India*. New Delhi: Manohar.

Abu-Lughod, J. L. (1989). *Before European Hegemony: The World System AD 1250–1350*. Oxford: Oxford University Press.

Allen, S. J. (1988). Trade, Transportation, and Tributaries: Exchange, Agriculture, and Settlement Distribution in Early Historic Period Kedah, Malaysia. Unpublished PhD thesis, University of Hawai'i at Manoa.

Andaya, L. Y. (1995). The Bugis-Makassar Diasporas. *Journal of the Malaysian Branch of the Royal Asiatic Society*, 68(1): 119–138.

(2008). *Leaves of the Same Tree*. Honolulu: University of Hawai'i Press.

ASEAN-COCI (ASEAN Committee for Culture and Information) (2006). Symposium on Maritime and Waterways, Muzium Negeri Terengganu, Terengganu, Malaysia, 23–28 January 2006. Unpublished proceedings.

Averbuch, B. D. (2013). From Siraf to Sumatra: Seafaring and Spices in the Islamicate Indo-Pacific, Ninth–Eleventh Centuries CE. Unpublished PhD thesis, Harvard University.

Baszley, B., Basrah, B. & Bala, B. (2009). *Arkeologi Maritim Borneo: Kajian di Tanjung Simpang Mengayau*. Kota Kinabalu: Universiti Malaysia Sabah.

Beavitt, P. (1992). Exotic Animal Products and Chinese Trade with Borneo. *Anthropozoologica*, 16: 181–188.

Bellina-Pryce, B. & Silapanth, P. (2006). Weaving Cultural Identities on Trans-Asiatic Networks: Upper Thai-Malay Peninsula – An Early Socio-Political Landscape. *Bulletin de l'École française d'Extrême-Orient*, 93: 257–293.

Bellwood, P. (1991). The Austronesian Dispersal and the Origin of Languages. *Scientific American*, 265(1): 88–93.

Benjamin, G. & Chou, C. (2002). *Tribal Communities in the Malay World: Historical, Cultural and Social Perspectives*. Singapore: Institute of Southeast Asian Studies.

Bielenstein, H. (2005). *Diplomacy and Trade in the Chinese World: 589–1276*. Leiden: Brill.

Bivar, A. D. H. (2000). *The Travels of Ibn Baṭṭūṭa, A.D. 1325–1354*. London: Hakluyt Society.

Blussé, L. (2013). Port Cities of South East Asia: 1400–1800. In *The Oxford Handbook of Cities in World History*. DOI: https://doi.org/10.1093/oxfordhb/9780199589531.013.0019.

Borschberg, P. (2004). *Iberians in the Singapore-Melaka Area and Adjacent Regions (16th to 18th Century)*. Wiesbaden: Harrassowitz Verlag.

Brindley, E. F. (2021). The Concept of "Educational Transformation" and Its Relationship to Civilizing Missions in Early China. *Journal of Chinese History* 中國歷史學刊, 5(1): 1–21.

Bronkhorst, J. (2011). The Spread of Sanskrit in Southeast Asia. In P.-Y. Manguin, A. Mani & G. Wade, eds., *Early Interactions between South and Southeast Asia: Reflections on Cross-Cultural Exchange*. Singapore: ISEAS Publishing, pp.263–276.

Bronson, B. (1977). Exchange at the Upstream and Downstream Ends: Notes toward a Functional Model of the Coastal State in Southeast Asia. In K. L. Hutterer, ed., *Economic Exchange and Social Interaction in Southeast Asia: Perspectives from Prehistory, History, and Ethnography*. Ann Arbor: Center for South and Southeast Asian Studies, The University of Michigan, pp. 39–52.

Brown, R. & Sjostrand, S. (2004). *Maritime Archaeology and Shipwreck Ceramics in Malaysia*. Kuala Lumpur: Department of Museums and Antiquities.

Bulbeck, D., Reid, A., Cheng, T. L. & Yiqi, W. (1998). *Southeast Asian Exports since the 14th Century: Cloves, Pepper, Coffee, and Sugar*. Singapore: Institute of Southeast Asian Studies.

Burkill, I. H. (1935). *A Dictionary of the Economic Products of the Malay Peninsula*. Oxford: Oxford University Press.

Cammanns, S. (1951). Chinese Carvings in Hornbill Ivory. *Sarawak Museum Journal*, 5: 393–399.

Carter, A. K. (2015). Beads, Exchange Networks and Emerging Complexity: A Case Study from Cambodia and Thailand (500 BCE–CE 500). *Cambridge Archaeological Journal*, 25(4): 733–757.

  (2016). The Production and Exchange of Glass and Stone Beads in Southeast Asia from 500 BCE to the Early Second Millennium CE: An Assessment of the Work of Peter Francis in Light of Recent Research. *Archaeological Research in Asia*, 6: 16–29.

Chaffee, J. W. (2018). *The Muslim Merchants of Premodern China: The History of a Maritime Asian Trade Diaspora, 750–1400*. Cambridge: Cambridge University Press.

Chandra, B. C. (1957). *Department of Archaeology, Annual Report on Indian Epigraphy for 1956–57*. New Delhi: Manager of Publications.

Chaudhuri, K. N. (2006). *The Trading World of Asia and the English East India Company: 1660–1760*. Cambridge: Cambridge University Press.

Chen, J. & Qian, J. (2000). *Zhufanzhi zhu pu*. Hong Kong: University of Hong Kong.

Chen, O. (2004). Ancient Singapore Earthenware Pottery. In J. N. Miksic & C. A. M. G. Low, eds., *Early Singapore, 1300s–1819: Evidence in Maps, Text and Artefacts*. Singapore: Singapore History Museum, pp. 55–72.

Chittick, A. (2020). *The Jiankang Empire in Chinese and World History*. New York: Oxford University Press.

Chong, A., Murphy, S. A. & Flecker, M. (2017). *The Tang Shipwreck: Art and Exchange in the 9th Century*. Singapore: Asian Civilisations Museum.

Chou, C. (2012). *The Orang Suku Laut of Riau, Indonesia*. London: Routledge.

Christie, J. W. (1998). The Medieval Tamil-Language Inscriptions in Southeast Asia and China. *Journal of Southeast Asian Studies*, 29(2): 239–268.

Clark, H. R. (2002). *Community, Trade, and Networks: Southern Fujian Province from the Third to the Thirteenth Century*. Cambridge: Cambridge University Press.

Coedes, G. (1918). Le royaume de Crivijaya. *Bulletin de l'École française d'Extrême-Orient*, 18(1): 1–36.

Cooke, N., Li, T. & Anderson, J. A. (2011). *The Tongking Gulf through History*. Philadelphia: University of Pennsylvania Press.

Daud, A. (2011). The Early Inscriptions of Indonesia and the Problem of the Sanskrit Cosmopolis. In P.-Y. Manguin, A. Mani & G. Wade, eds., *Early Interactions between South and Southeast Asia: Reflections on Cross-Cultural Exchange*. Singapore: ISEAS Publishing, pp.277–298.

Deng, G. (1999). *Maritime Sector, Institutions, and Sea Power of Premodern China*. Westport, CT: Greenwood Press.

Deng, G. & Kang, T. (1997). *Chinese Maritime Activities and Socioeconomic Development, c. 2100 BC–1900 AD*. Westport, CT: Greenwood Press.

Devahuti, D. (1965). *India and Ancient Malaya, from the Earliest Times to circa AD 1400*. Singapore: Eastern Universities Press.

Donkin, R. A. (1999). *Dragon's Brain Perfume: An Historical Geography of Camphor*. Leiden: Brill.

Drechsler, W. (2013). Wang Anshi and the Origins of Modern Public Management in Song Dynasty China. *Public Money & Management*, 33(5): 353–360.

Druce, S. C. (2009). *The Lands West of the Lakes: A History of the Ajattappareng Kingdoms of South Sulawesi, 1200 to 1600 CE*. Leiden: Brill.

Elvin, M. (2008). *The Retreat of the Elephants*. New Haven, CT: Yale University Press.

Flecker, M. (2000). A 9th-century Arab or Indian Shipwreck in Indonesian Waters. *International Journal of Nautical Archaeology*, 29(2): 199–217.

(2001). A Ninth-Century AD Arab or Indian Shipwreck in Indonesia: First Evidence for Direct Trade with China. *World Archaeology*, 32(3): 335–354.

(2002). *The Archaeological Excavation of the 10th Century: Intan Shipwreck.* British Archaeological Reports, Vol. 1047. Oxford: Archaeopress.

(2007). The South-China-Sea Tradition: The Hybrid Hulls of South-East Asia. *International Journal of Nautical Archaeology*, 36(1): 75–90.

(2022). The Temasik Wreck (Mid-14th Century), Singapore Preliminary Report. *Temasik Working Paper Series*, no. 4.

Francis, P. (1990). Glass Beads in Asia Part Two: Indo-Pacific Beads. *Asian Perspectives*, 29(1): 1–23.

(1991). Beads in Indonesia. *Asian Perspectives*, 30(2): 217–241.

Gaur, A. (2011). Marine Archaeological Investigations along the Tamil Nadu Coast and Their Implications for Understanding Cultural Expansion to Southeast Asian Countries. In P.-Y. Manguin, A. Mani & G. Wade, eds., *Early Interactions between South and Southeast Asia: Reflections on Cross-Cultural Exchange*. Singapore: Institute of Southeast Asian Studies, pp. 221–240.

Gaur, A. S., Muthucumarana, R., Chandraratne, W. M., et al. (2011). Preliminary Assessment of an Early Historic (2000-year-old) Shipwreck at Godawaya, Sri Lanka. *Journal of the Australasian Institute for Maritime Archaeology*, 35: 9–17.

Ge, Y. & Linduff, K. M. (1990). Sanxingdui: A New Bronze Age Site in Southwest China. *Antiquity*, 64(244): 505–513.

国家文物局水下文化遗产保护中心等编著 [Guojia wenwuju shuixia wenhua yanchang baihu zhongxin et al.] (2017). 南海Ⅰ号沉船考古报告之二: *2014–2015[Second Archeological Report of the Shipwreck Nanhai 1: 2014–2015].*年发掘. 北京 [Beijing]: 文物出版社 [Wenwu chubanshe].

Guy, J. (2012). Tamil Merchants and the Hindu-Buddhist Diaspora in Early Southeast Asia. In P.-Y. Manguin, A. Mani & G. Wade, eds., *Early Interactions between South and Southeast Asia: Reflections on Cross-Cultural Exchange*. Singapore: Institute of Southeast Asian Studies, pp.243–262.

(2017). The Phanom Surin Shipwreck, a Pahlavi Inscription, and Their Significance for the Early History of Lower Central Thailand. *The Journal of the Siam Society*, 105: 179–196.

Hall, K. R. (1978). International Trade and Foreign Diplomacy in Early Medieval South India. *Journal of the Economic and Social History of the Orient*, 21(1): 75–98.

(1996). The Textile Industry in Southeast Asia, 1400–1800. *Journal of the Economic and Social History of the Orient*, 39(2): 87–135.

(2001). Upstream and Downstream Unification in Southeast Asia's First Islamic Polity: The Changing Sense of Community in the Fifteenth Century "Hikayat Raja-Raja Pasai" Court Chronicle. *Journal of the Economic and Social History of the Orient*, 44(2): 198–229.

(2003). *Trade and Statecraft in the Ages of Colas*. New Delhi: Abhinav Publications.

(2006). Maritime Diasporas in the Indian Ocean and East and Southeast Asia (960–1775). *Journal of the Economic and Social History of the Orient*, 49(4): 381–534.

(2009). Ports-of-Trade, Maritime Diasporas, and Networks of Trade and Cultural Integration in the Bay of Bengal Region of the Indian Ocean: c. 1300–1500. *Journal of the Economic and Social History of the Orient*, 53(1–2): 109–145.

(2011a). *A History of Early Southeast Asia Maritime Trade and Societal Development, 100–1500*. Lanham, MD: Rowman & Littlefield.

(2011b). Java's Evolving Military History in the Tenth to the Fifteenth Centuries: Evidence of Contemporary Iron Imports and their Consequence as Documented in Shipwrecks, Epigraphy, and Literary Records. Unpublished paper presented at the Association for Asian Studies Annual Meeting, Honolulu, Hawai'i.

Halley, E. (1686). An Historical Account of the Trade Winds, and Monsoons, Observable in the Seas between and near the Tropicks, with an Attempt to Assign the Physical Cause of the Said Wind. *Philosophical Transactions of the Royal Society*, 16: 153–168.

Hefner, R. W. (1990). *The Political Economy of Mountain Java*. Berkeley: University of California Press.

Hein, D. D. L. (2001). The Sawankhalok Ceramic Industry. Unpublished PhD dissertation, Deakin University.

Hendrickson, M. (2010). Historic Routes to Angkor: Development of the Khmer Road System (Ninth to Thirteenth Centuries AD) in Mainland Southeast Asia. *Antiquity*, 84(324): 480–496.

Heng, D. (1999). Temasik as an International and Regional Trading Port in the Thirteenth and Fourteenth Centuries: A Reconstruction Based on Recent Archaeological Data. *Journal of the Malaysian Branch of the Royal Asiatic Society*, 72(1): 113–124.

(2001). The Trade in Lakawood Products between South China and the Malay world from the Twelfth to Fifteenth Centuries AD. *Journal of Southeast Asian Studies*, 32(2): 133–149.

(2002). Reconstructing Banzu, a Fourteenth-Century Port Settlement in Singapore. *Journal of the Malaysian Branch of the Royal Asiatic Society*, 75(1): 69–90.

(2006). Shipping, Customs Procedures, and the Foreign Community: The "Pingzhou ketan" on Aspects of Guangzhou's Maritime Economy in the Late Eleventh Century. *Journal of Song-Yuan Studies*, (38): 1–38.

(2008). Structures, Networks and Commercial Practices of Private Chinese Maritime Traders in Island Southeast Asia in the Early Second Millennium AD. *International Journal of Maritime History*, 20(2): 27–54.

(2012). *Sino-Malay Trade and Diplomacy from the Tenth through the Fourteenth Century.* Singapore: ISEAS Press.

(2013). Trans-Regionalism and Economic Co-Dependency in the South China Sea: The Case of China and the Malay Region (10th–14th centuries AD). *International History Review*, 35(3): 486–510.

(2015). Southeast Asian Primary Products in China and Their Impact on Chinese Material Culture in the Tenth to Seventeenth Centuries. In V. Mair & L. Kelley, eds., *China and Its Southern Neighbours*. Singapore: ISEAS Press, pp. 214–238.

(2017). The Tang Shipwreck and the Nature of China's Maritime Trade during the Late Tang Period. In A. Chong, S. A. Murphy & M. Flecker, eds., *The Tang Shipwreck: Art and Exchange in the 9th Century*. Singapore: National Heritage Board, pp.142–159.

(2018). Ships, Shipwrecks, and Archaeological Recoveries as Sources of Southeast Asian History. In *Oxford Research Encyclopedia of Asian History*. https://oxfordre.com/asianhistory/view/10.1093/acrefore/9780190277727.001.0001/acrefore-9780190277727-e-97.

(2019a). State-Formation and Socio-political Structure of the Malay Coastal Region in the Late Thirteenth to Early Fifteenth Centuries. In K. R. Hall, S. Ghosh, K. Gangopadhyay & R. Mukherjee, eds., *Cross-Cultural Networking in the Eastern Indian Ocean Realm, c. 100–1800*. Delhi: Primus Books, pp. 203–228.

(2019b). Regional Influences, Economic Adaptation and Cultural Articulation: Diversity and Cosmopolitanism in Fourteenth-Century Singapore. *Journal of Southeast Asian Studies*, 50(4): 476–488.

Heng, G. (2019). An Ordinary Ship and Its Stories of Early Globalism: World Travel, Mass Production, and Art in the Global Middle Ages. *Journal of Medieval Worlds*, 1(1): 11–54.

Higham, C. (1996). *The Bronze Age of Southeast Asia*. Cambridge: Cambridge University Press.

Hirth, F. & Rockhill, W. W. (1970). *Chau Ju-kua: His Work on the Chinese and Arab Trade in the Twelfth and Thirteenth Centuries, Entitled Chu-Fan-Chï*. Taipei: Cheng-wen.

Ho, C. M. (2001). The Ceramic Boom in Minnan during Song and Yuan Times. In A. Schottenhammer, ed., *The Emporium of the World: Maritime Quanzhou, 1000–1400*. Leiden: Brill, pp. 237–282.

黄纯艳 [Huang, C. Y.] (2003). *Songdai haiwai maoyi* 宋代海外贸易 [*Maritime Trade of the Song Dynasty*]. Beijing: 社会科学文献出版社 [Shehui kexue wenxian chubanshe].

Hudson, B. & Lustig, T. (2008). Communities of the Past: A New View of the Old Walls and Hydraulic System at Sriksetra, Myanmar (Burma). *Journal of Southeast Asian Studies*, 39(2): 269–296.

Irwin, D. A. (1991). Mercantilism as Strategic Trade Policy: The Anglo-Dutch Rivalry for the East India Trade. *Journal of Political Economy*, 99(6): 1296–1314.

Jacq-Hergoualc'h, M. (2002). *The Malay Peninsula: Crossroads of the Maritime Silk Road (100 BC–1300 AD)*. Leiden: Brill.

Jahan, S. H. (2006). *Excavating Waves and Winds of (Ex)change: A Study of Maritime Trade in Early Bengal*. British Archaeological Reports International Series no. 5. Oxford: Archaeopress.

Karashima, N. (2009). South Indian Merchant Guilds in the Indian Ocean and Southeast Asia. In H. Kulke, K. Kesavapany & V. Sakhuja, eds., *Nagapattinam to Suvarnadwipa: Reflections on the Chola Naval Expeditions to Southeast Asia*. Singapore: ISEAS Publishing, pp. 135–157.

Khakzad, S. (2012). Siraf Archaeological Report. *Sasanika Archaeology*, 5: 1–8.

King, V. T. & Druce, S. C. (2020). Brunei Darussalam: Origins, Early History and Social Structure: A Celebration and Evaluation of the Work of Professor Donald E. Brown. In V. T. King and S. C. Druce, eds., *Origins, History and Social Structure in Brunei Darussalam*. Abingdon: Routledge, pp. 1–9.

Krahl, R. (2010). *Shipwrecked: Tang Treasures and Monsoon Winds*. Washington, D.C.: Smithsonian Books.

Kulke, H. (1993). "Kadātuan Śrīvijaya" – Empire or Kraton of Śrīvijaya? A Reassessment of the Epigraphical Evidence. *Bulletin de l'École française d'Extrême-Orient*, 80(1): 159–180.

    (2009). The Naval Expeditions of the Cholas in the Context of Asian History. In H. Kulke, K. Kesavapany & V. Sakhuja, eds., *Nagapattinam to Suvarnadwipa: Reflections on the Chola Naval Expeditions to Southeast Asia*. Singapore: ISEAS Publishing, pp.1–19.

Kulke, H., Kesavapany, K. & Sakhuja, V. (2009). *Nagapattinam to Suvarnadwipa: Reflections on the Chola Naval Expeditions to Southeast Asia*. Singapore: ISEAS Publishing.

Kuwabara J. (1928). P'u Shou-keng, a Man of the Western Regions, Who Was Superintendent of the Trading Ships Office in Ch'uan-chou towards the End of the Sung Dynasty. *Memoirs of the Research Department of the Toyo Bunko*, 2: 1–79; 7: 1–104.

Kwa, C. G., Heng, D., Borschberg, P. & Tan, T.Y. (2019). *Seven Hundred Years: A History of Singapore.* Singapore: Marshall Cavendish International Asia.

Kwee, H. K. (2006). *The Political Economy of Java's Northeast Coast, c. 1740–1800: Elite Synergy.* Leiden: Brill.

——— (2013). Chinese Economic Dominance in Southeast Asia: A Longue Duree Perspective. *Comparative Studies in Society and History*, 55(1): 5–34.

Laidley, J. W. (1848). Notes of the Inscriptions from Singapur and Province Wellesley Forwarded by the Hon. Col. Butterworth, C. B. and Col. J. Low. *Journal of the Asiatic Society of Bengal*, 17(11): 66–72.

Lamb, A. (1964). A Visit to Siraf, an Ancient Port on the Persian Gulf. *Journal of the Malaysian Branch of the Royal Asiatic Society*, 37(1): 1–19.

Lavy, P. (2003). As in Heaven, So on Earth: The Politics of Visnu, Śiva and Harihara Images in Preangkorian Khmer Civilisation. *Journal of Southeast Asian Studies*, 34(1): 21–39.

Lawler, A. (2014). Seafaring in Ancient Sri Lanka. *Archaeology*, 67(6): 42–47.

Legge, J. (1886). *A Record of Buddhistic Kingdoms; Being an Account by the Chinese Monk Fâ-Hien of His Travels in India and Ceylon, A.D. 399-414, In Search of the Buddhist Books of Discipline. Translated and Annotated with a Corean Recension of the Chinese Text.* Oxford: Clarendon Press.

Li, H. L. (1979). *Nan-Fang Ts' ao-Mu Chuang: A Fourth Century Flora of Southeast Asia.* Hong Kong: The Chinese University Press.

Li, T. (2006). The Rise and Fall of the Jiaozhi Ocean Region. In A. Schottenhammer & R. Ptak, eds., *The Perception of Maritime Space in Traditional Chinese Sources.* Wiesbaden: Harrassowitz Verlag, pp. 125–140.

Liebner, H. H. (2014). *The Siren of Cirebon: A Tenth-Century Trading Vessel Lost in the Java Sea.* Unpublished PhD dissertation, University of Leeds.

Lim, T. S. (2012). *14th Century Singapore: The Temasek Paradigm.* Unpublished MA dissertation, National University of Singapore.

Lorrillard, M. (2014). Pre-Angkorian Communities in the Middle Mekong Valley (Laos and Adjacent Areas). In S. Murphy & N. Revire, eds., *Before Siam: Essays in Art and Archaeology.* Bangkok: River Books and the Siam Society, pp. 186–215.

羅香林 [Luo, X. L.] (1955). *Pu Shou Geng Zhuan* 蒲寿庚传 [*Biography of Pu Shou Geng*]. 台北 [Taibei]:中华文化出版事业委员会 [Zhonghua wen-hua chuban shiye weiyuanhui].

Lustig, E. J. (2009). *Power and Pragmatism in the Political Economy of Angkor*. Unpublished PhD dissertation, University of Sydney.

Mabbett, I. & Chandler, D. (1995). *The Khmers*. Oxford: Blackwell Publishers.

Manguin, P. Y. (1993). Trading Ships of the South China Sea: Shipbuilding Techniques and Their Role in the History of the Development of Asian Trade Networks. *Journal of the Economic and Social History of the Orient*, 36(3): 253–280.

(1996). Southeast Asian Shipping in the Indian Ocean during the 1st Millennium AD. In H. P. Ray & J.-F. Salles, eds., *Tradition and Archaeology: Early Maritime Contacts in the Indian Ocean*. Lyon: Manohar/Maison de l'Orient Méditerranéen, pp. 181–198.

(2009). Southeast Sumatra in Protohistoric and Srivijaya Times: Upstream-Downstream Relations and the Settlement of the Peneplain. In D. Bonatz, J. Miksic, J. D. Neidel & M. L. Tjoa-Bonatz, eds., *From Distant Tales: Archaeology and Ethnohistory in the Highlands of Sumatra*. Newcastle upon Tyne: Cambridge Scholars, pp. 434–484.

(2014). Early Coastal States of Southeast Asia: Funan and Śrīvijaya. In J. Guy, ed., *Lost Kingdoms: Hindu-Buddhist Sculpture of Early Southeast Asia*. New York: Metropolitan Museum of Art, pp. 111–115.

(2019). Sewn Boats of Southeast Asia: The Stitched-Plank and Lashed-Lug Tradition. *International Journal of Nautical Archaeology*, 48(2): 400–415.

Masaki, M. (2010). Contacts between Empires and Entrepots and the Role of Supra-regional Network: Song-Yuan-Ming Transition of the Maritime Asia, 960–1405. In *Empires, Systems, and Maritime Networks*, Working Paper Series, no. 01, Osaka University, pp. 1–24.

Mathers, W. M. & Flecker, M. (1997). *Archaeological Report: Archaeological Recovery of the Java Sea Wreck*. Annapolis: Pacific Sea Resources.

McGrail, S. (2004). *Boats of the World: From the Stone Age to Medieval Times*. Oxford: Oxford University Press.

McKinnon, E. E. (1977). Research at Kota Cina, a Sung-Yuan Period Trading Site in East Sumatra., *Archipel*, 14: 19–32.

(2009). Ceramics, Cloth, Iron and Salt: Coastal Hinterland Interaction in the Karo Region of Northeastern Sumatra. In D. Bonatz, J. Miksic, J. D. Neidel & M. L. Tjoa-Bonatz, eds., *From Distant Tales: Archaeology and Ethnohistory in the Highlands of Sumatra*. Newcastle upon Tyne: Cambridge Scholars, pp. 120–142.

(2018). Buddhism and the Pre-Islamic Archaeology of Kutei in the Mahakam Valley of East Kalimantan. In N. A. Taylor, ed., *Studies in Southeast Asian Art: Essays in Honor of Stanley J. O'Connor*. Ithaca, NY: Cornell University Press, pp. 217–240.

Meenakshisundararajan, A. (2009). Rajendra Chola's Naval Expedition and the Chola Trade with Southeast and East Asia. In H. Kulke, K. Kesavapany & V. Sakhuja, eds., *Nagapattinam to Suvarnadwipa: Reflections on the Chola Naval Expeditions to Southeast Asia*. Singapore: ISEAS Publishing, pp. 168–177.

Merwin, D. (1977). Selections from Wen-Wu on the Excavation of a Sung Dynasty Seagoing Vessel in Ch'uan-Chou. *Chinese Sociology and Anthropology*, 9(3): 1–106.

Miksic, J. N. (1994). Recently Discovered Chinese Green Glazed Wares of the Thirteenth and Fourteenth Centuries in Singapore and the Riau Islands. In H. Chuimei, ed., *New Light on Chinese Yue and Longquan Wares*. Hong Kong: University of Hong Kong, pp. 229–250.

(2003). *Earthenware in Southeast Asia: Proceedings of the Singapore Symposium on Premodern Southeast Asian Earthenwares*. Singapore: NUS Press.

(2009). Highland-Lowland Connections in Jambi, South Sumatra, and West Sumatra, 11th to 14th Centuries. In D. Bonatz, D., J. Miksic & J. D. Neidel, eds., *From Distant Tales: Archaeology and Ethnohistory in the Highlands of Sumatra*. Newcastle upon Tyne: Cambridge Scholars, pp. 75–102.

(2013). *Singapore and the Silk Road of the Sea, 1300–1800*. Singapore: NUS Press.

Mudar, K. M. (1999). How Many Dvaravati Kingdoms? Locational Analysis of First Millennium AD Moated Settlements in Central Thailand. *Journal of Anthropological Archaeology*, 18(1): 1–28.

Mullins, D. A., Hoyer, D., Collins, C., et al. (2018). A Systematic Assessment of "Axial Age" Proposals Using Global Comparative Historical Evidence. *American Sociological Review*, 83(3): 596–626.

Murphy, S. A. (2018). Revisiting the Bujang Valley: A Southeast Asian Entrepôt Complex on the Maritime Trade Route. *Journal of the Royal Asiatic Society*, 28(2): 355–389.

Muthucumarana, R., Gaur, A. S., Chandraratne, W. M., et al. (2014). An Early Historic Assemblage Offshore of Godawaya, Sri Lanka: Evidence for Early Regional Seafaring in South Asia. *Journal of Maritime Archaeology*, 9(1): 41–58.

Myo, N., Kyaw, M. W., Moore, E., Win, K. & Win, M. (2017). Pinle (Maingmaw): Research at an Ancient Pyu City. Nalanda–Sriwijaya Centre Archaeology Unit Archaeology Report Series No 6. Singapore: Nalanda-Sriwijaya Centre.

Nanhai No. 1 (2011). Guangdong sheng wen wu kao gu yan jiu suo 广东省文物考古研究所. *2011 nian "Nanhai No.1" de kao gu fa jue* 2011年"南海一号"的考古试掘 [The 2011 Excavation Report of Nanhai No. 1]. Beijing: Ke xue chu ban she.

Nanhai No. 1 (2018). Guangdongsheng wenwu kaogu yanjiusuo 广东省文物考古研究所, Guojia wenwuju shuixia wenhua yichan baohu zhongxin 国家文物局水下文化遗产保护中心, Guangdongsheng bowuguan 广东省博物馆, Guangdong haishang sichou zhi lu bowuguan 广东海上丝绸之路博物馆. 2018. *Nanhai No. 1 chen chuan kao gu bao gao zhi er –2014~2015 nian fajue* 南海I号沉船考古报告之二——2014~2015年发掘 [The 2014–2015 Excavation Report of Nanhai No. 1]. Beijing: Wenwu chubanshe.

Nik, H. S. (1994). *Art, Archaeology and the Early Kingdoms in the Malay Peninsula and Sumatra: c.400–1400 A.D.* Unpublished PhD dissertation, University of London.

Nishino, N., Aoyama, T., Kimura, J., Nogami, T. and Thi Lien, L. Nishimura Project: The Oldest Shipwreck Found in Vietnam: Testimony to the Maritime Ceramic Route. Paper presented at Underwater Archaeology in Vietnam and Southeast Asia: Co-Operation for Development, Quang Ngai, Vietnam.

Peacock, B. A. V. (1970). New Light on the Ancient Settlements in Kedah and Province Wellesley. *Malaysia in History*, 13(2): 20–27.

Phuong, T. K. (2009). The Architecture of the Temple-Towers of Ancient Champa (Central Vietnam) 1. In A. Hardy, M. Cucarzi and P. Zolese, eds., *Champa and the Archaeology of My Son (Vietnam)*. Singapore: NUS Press, pp. 155–186.

Possehl, G. L. (1982). *The Indus Civilization: A Contemporary Perspective*. New Delhi: IBH.

Potts, D. T. (2009). The Archaeology and Early History of the Persian Gulf. In L. G. Potter, ed., *The Persian Gulf in History*. New York: Palgrave Macmillan, pp. 27–56. https://doi.org/10.1057/9780230618459_2.

Ptak, R. (1995). Images of Maritime Asia in Two Yuan Texts: "Daoyi zhilue" and "Yiyu zhi". *Journal of Song-Yuan Studies*, 25: 47–75.

Quaritch-Wales, D. C. & Quaritch-Wales, H. G. (1947). Further Work on Indian Sites in Malaya. *Journal of the Malayan Branch of the Royal Asiatic Society*, 20(1): 1–11.

Ray, H. P. (1989). Early Maritime Contacts between South and Southeast Asia. *Journal of Southeast Asian Studies*, 20(1): 42–54.

(1990). Seafaring in the Bay of Bengal in the Early Centuries AD. *Studies in History*, 6(1): 1–14.

Revire, N. (2014). Glimpses of Buddhist Practices and Rituals in Dvāravatī and Its Neighbouring Cultures. In N. Revire and S. A. Murphy, eds., *Before Siam: Essays in Art and Archaeology.* Bangkok: River Books, pp. 241–271.

Ricklefs, M. C. (2010). *A New History of Southeast Asia.* Basingstoke: Palgrave Macmillan.

Ridho, A. & McKinnon, E. E. (1998). *The Pulau Buaya Wreck: Finds from the Song Period.* Jakarta: Ceramic Society of Indonesia.

Rooney, D. F. (2003). Kendi in the Cultural Context of Southeast Asia: A Commentary. *SPAFA Journal* (Old Series 1991–2013), 13(2): 5–16.

Salemink, O. (2008). Trading Goods, Prestige and Power: A Revisionist History of Lowlander-Highlander Relations in Vietnam. In P. Boomgaard, D. Kooiman & H. Schulte Nordholt, eds., *Linking Destinies: Trade, Towns and Kin in Asian History.* Leiden: Brill, pp. 51–69.

Sarip, M. (2020). Kajian Etimologis Kerajaan (Kutai) Martapura di Muara Kaman, Kalimantan Timur. *Yupa: Historical Studies Journal*, 4(2): 50–61.

Sastri, K. N. (1949). Takuapa and Its Tamil Inscription. *Journal of the Malayan Branch of the Royal Asiatic Society*, 22(1): 25–30.

Schafer, E. H. (1963). *The Golden Peaches of Samarkand.* Berkeley: University of California Press.

Schottenhammer, A. (2016). China's Gate to the Indian Ocean: Iranian and Arab Long-Distance Traders. *Harvard Journal of Asiatic Studies*, 76(1): 135–179.

Schurmann, F. (1967). *Economic Structure of the Yüan Dynasty: Translation of Chapters 93 and 94 of the "Yüan Shih."* Cambridge, MA: Harvard University Press.

Sen, T. (2003). *Buddhism, Diplomacy, and Trade: The Realignment of Sino-Indian Relations, 600–1400.* Honolulu: University of Hawai'i Press.

Shiro, M. (1998). Dai Viet and the South China Sea Trade: From the 10th to the 15th Century. *Crossroads: An Interdisciplinary Journal of Southeast Asian Studies*, 12(1): 1–34.

Sidebotham, S. E. (2011). *Berenike and the Ancient Maritime Spice Route.* Berkeley: University of California Press.

Smail, J. R. (1961). On an Autonomous History of Southeast Asia. *Journal of Southeast Asian History*, 2(1): 77–102.

So, B. K. L. (2000). *Prosperity, Region, and Institutions in Maritime China: The South Fukien Pattern, 946–1368.* Cambridge, MA: Harvard University Asia Center.

Sopher, D. E. (1977). *The Sea Nomads: A Study of the Maritime Boat People of Southeast Asia*. Singapore: National Museum.

Stadtner, D. M. & Freeman, M. (2013). *Ancient Pagan: Buddhist Plain of Merit*. Bangkok: River Books.

苏继顾 [Su, J.]. (1981). *Daoyi zhilüe jiaoshi* 岛夷志略校释 [Annotated treatise of the Barbarian Isles]. Beijing: 中华书局 [Zhonghua shuju].

Subbarayalu, Y. (2009). Anjuvannam: A Maritime Trade Guild of Medieval Times. In H. Kulke, K. Kesavapany & V. Sakhuja, eds., *Nagapattinam to Suvarnadwipa: Reflections on the Chola Naval Expeditions to Southeast Asia*. Singapore: ISEAS Publishing, pp. 158–167.

Takakusu, J. (1966). *The Buddhist Religion as Practiced in India and the Malay Archipelago by I-Tsing*. Delhi: Mushiram Manoharlal.

Tallet, P. (2016). The Egyptians on the Red Sea Shore During the Pharaonic Era. In M.-F. Boussac, J.-F. Salles & J.-B. Yon, eds., *Ports of the Ancient Indian Ocean*. Delhi: Primus Books, pp. 3–19.

Tambiah, S. J. (1977). The Galactic Polity: The Structure of Traditional Kingdoms in Southeast Asia. *Annals of the New York Academy of Sciences*, 293(1): 69–97.

Tana, L. (2006). A View from the Sea: Perspectives on the Northern and Central Vietnamese Coast. *Journal of Southeast Asian Studies*, 37(1): 83–102.

Taylor, K. W. (1999). The Early Kingdoms. In N. Tarling, ed., *The Cambridge History of Southeast Asia Vol. 1 Part 1, From Early Times to c. 1500*. Cambridge: Cambridge University Press, pp. 137–182.

Tibbetts, G. R. (1979). *A Study of the Arabic Texts Containing Material on South-East Asia*. Leiden: Brill.

Tripati, S. (2017). Seafaring Archaeology of the East Coast of India and Southeast Asia during the Early Historical Period. *Ancient Asia*, 8: 1–22.

Vallibhotama, S. (1986). Political and Cultural Continuities at Dvaravati Sites. In D. G. Marr & A. C. Milner, eds., *Southeast Asia in the 9th to 14th Centuries*. Singapore: Institute of Southeast Asian Studies, pp. 229–238.

Verma, V. K. (2005). Maritime Trade between Early Historic Tamil Nadu and Southeast Asia. *Proceedings of the Indian History Congress*, 66: 125–134.

Wade, G. (2009). An Early Age of Commerce in Southeast Asia, 900–1300 CE. *Journal of Southeast Asian Studies*, 40(2): 221–265.

    (2010). Early Muslim Expansion in South-East Asia, Eighth to Fifteenth Centuries. In D. O. Morgan & A. Reid, eds., *The New Cambridge History of Islam. Vol. 3*. Cambridge: Cambridge University Press, pp. 366–408.

    (2019). Southeast Asia in the Fifteenth Century: Early Modern or What? In S. Kumar, S. P. Mohanty, A. Kumar & R. Kumar, eds., *China, India and Alternative Asian Modernities*. New Delhi: Routledge, pp. 121–141.

Wang, G. (2003). *The Nanhai Trade: Early Chinese Trade in the South China Sea*. Singapore: Eastern Universities Press.

Watson-Andaya, B. (1993). Cash Cropping and Upstream Downstream Tensions: The Case of Jambi in the Seventeenth and Eighteenth Centuries. In A. Reid, ed., *Southeast Asia in the Early Modern Era: Trade, Power and Belief*. Ithaca, NY: Cornell University Press, pp. 91–122.

Wheatley, P. (1959). Geographical Notes on Some Commodities Involved in Sung Maritime Trade. *Journal of the Malayan Branch of the Royal Asiatic Society*, 32(2): 1–140.

(1961). *The Golden Khersonese: Studies in the Historical Geography of the Malay Peninsula before A. D. 1500*. Westport, CT: Greenwood Press.

(1964). *Impressions of the Malay Peninsula in Ancient Times*. Singapore: Eastern Universities Press.

Whitehouse, D. (1985). Abbasid Maritime Trade: Archaeology and the Age of Expansion. *Rivista degli studi orientali*, 59: 339–347.

Williamson, H. R. (1935). *Wang An Shih: A Chinese Statesman and Educationalist of the Sung Dynasty, Vol. 1*. London: A. Probsthain.

Wink, A. (1990). *Al-Hind: The Making of the Indo-Islamic World. Volume 1: Early Medieval India and the Expansion of Islam, 7–11th Centuries*. Delhi: Oxford University Press.

(1997). *Al-Hind, Volume 2: Slave Kings and the Islamic Conquest, 11th–13th Centuries*. Leiden: Brill.

Wolters, O. W. (1967). *Early Indonesian Commerce: A Study of the Origins of Srivijaya*. Ithaca, NY: Cornell University Press.

(1999). *History, Culture, and Region in Southeast Asian Perspectives*. Ithaca, NY: Cornell University Press.

Zhou, Q. & Tu, Y. (1996). *Ling wai dai da / Zhou Qufei zhu; Tu Youxiang jiao zhu*. Shanghai: Yuan dong chu ban she.

Cambridge Elements ☰

The Global Middle Ages

Geraldine Heng
University of Texas at Austin

Geraldine Heng is Perceval Professor of English and Comparative Literature at the University of Texas, Austin. She is the author of *The Invention of Race in the European Middle Ages* (2018) and *England and the Jews: How Religion and Violence Created the First Racial State in the West* (2018), both published by Cambridge University Press, as well as *Empire of Magic: Medieval Romance and the Politics of Cultural Fantasy* (2003, Columbia). She is the editor of *Teaching the Global Middle Ages* (2022, MLA), coedits the University of Pennsylvania Press series, RaceB4Race: Critical Studies of the Premodern, and is working on a new book, Early Globalisms: The Interconnected World, 500–1500 CE. Originally from Singapore, Heng is a Fellow of the Medieval Academy of America, a member of the Medievalists of Color, and Founder and Co-director, with Susan Noakes, of the Global Middle Ages Project: www.globalmiddleages.org.

Susan Noakes
University of Minnesota, Twin Cities

Susan Noakes is Professor and Chair of French and Italian at the University of Minnesota, Twin Cities. From 2002 to 2008 she was Director of the Center for Medieval Studies; she has also served as Director of Italian Studies, Director of the Center for Advanced Feminist Studies, and Associate Dean for Faculty in the College of Liberal Arts. Her publications include *The Comparative Perspective on Literature: Essays in Theory and Practice* (co-edited with Clayton Koelb, Cornell, 1988) and *Timely Reading: Between Exegesis and Interpretation* (Cornell, 1988), along with many articles and critical editions in several areas of French, Italian, and neo-Latin Studies. She is the Founder and Co-director, with Geraldine Heng, of the Global Middle Ages Project: www.globalmiddleages.org.

About the Series

Elements in the Global Middle Ages is a series of concise studies that introduce researchers and instructors to an uncentered, interconnected world, c. 500–1500 CE. Individual Elements focus on the globe's geographic zones, its natural and built environments, its cultures, societies, arts, technologies, peoples, ecosystems, and lifeworlds.

Cambridge Elements ☰

The Global Middle Ages

Printed in the United States
by Baker & Taylor Publisher Services